"*Eight Stories Up* is a powerful and important book. It offers hope to those without it and provides clear, practical suggestions for individuals and family members whose lives are hit by suicidal despair. I cannot recommend this book highly enough."

—*Kay Redfield Jamison, Ph.D., Professor of Psychiatry,*
Johns Hopkins School of Medicine and author of An Unquiet Mind

"For those of us who have gotten caught in the rip current of depression, *Eight Stories Up* is a tether, a lifeline, with which we can begin to pull ourselves back to shore."

—*Brent Runyon, author of* The Burn Journals

"Interspersed with the poignant and personal experience of his own near-suicide, Lezine offers education and hope for others who may be thinking of ending their lives."

—*Bev Cobain, author of* When Nothing Matters Anymore:
A Survival Guide for Depressed Teens *and* Dying to Be Free:
A Healing Guide for Families after a Suicide

"A candid account of life's trials and hopes, *Eight Stories Up* is an engaging narrative perfect for any adolescent who may feel lost or alone. Infused with facts and resources, DeQuincy Lezine's gripping story of his depressed adolescence and chronicle of recovery brings us into his world and lets us all know we're not alone. With an honest view of his life and experiences, Lezine teaches all adolescents how to choose hope over suicide."

—*Alison K. Malmon, Founder and Executive Director, Active Minds, Inc.*

"*Eight Stories Up* is a practical, useful, and compelling book that should be in every high school library and on every therapist's shelf. Lezine and Brent have taken the complex, multifaceted problem of suicide and put it into language and examples that everyone can benefit from. *Eight Stories Up* clears up the confusion about suicide, answers the questions so many have, and sheds light on the practical, real-life struggle of one teen who overcame the demons, myths, and horrors of mental illness. As you walk through the author's life in this book, you will relate, learn, and develop your own insights to help get you through. What a fabulous book of hope and inspiration for anyone who feels their life might be over. Read *Eight Stories Up* and you will know that it is not!"

—*Daniel J. Reidenberg, Psy.D., FAPA, Executive Director,*
Suicide Awareness Voices of Education (SAVE), and Fellow,
American Psychotherapy Association

"Quix's direct experience as a suicide attempter, combined with his Ph.D. education in psychological research, provides a unique perspective from which parents and professionals working with struggling teens can gain insight and understanding into the complex world of a suicidal mind."

—*Sue Blauner, author of* How I Stayed Alive When My Brain Was
Trying to Kill Me: One Person's Guide to Suicide Prevention

THE
ANNENBERG FOUNDATION TRUST
AT
SUNNYLANDS

The Annenberg Foundation Trust at Sunnylands'
Adolescent Mental Health Initiative

Patrick E. Jamieson, Ph.D., *series editor*

Eight Stories Up

An Adolescent Chooses Hope Over Suicide

DeQuincy A. Lezine, Ph.D.

with David Brent, M.D.

OXFORD
UNIVERSITY PRESS
2008

OXFORD

UNIVERSITY PRESS

Oxford University Press, Inc., publishes works that further
Oxford University's objective of excellence
in research, scholarship, and education.

The Annenberg Foundation Trust at Sunnylands
The Annenberg Public Policy Center of the University of Pennsylvania
Oxford University Press

Oxford   New York
Auckland   Cape Town   Dar es Salaam   Hong Kong   Karachi
Kuala Lumpur   Madrid   Melbourne   Mexico City   Nairobi
New Delhi   Shanghai   Taipei   Toronto

With offices in
Argentina   Austria   Brazil   Chile   Czech Republic   France   Greece
Guatemala   Hungary   Italy   Japan   Poland   Portugal   Singapore
South Korea   Switzerland   Thailand   Turkey   Ukraine   Vietnam

Copyright © 2008 by Oxford University Press, Inc.

Published by Oxford University Press, Inc.
198 Madison Avenue, New York, New York 10016

www.oup.com

Oxford is a registered trademark of Oxford University Press

Library of Congress Cataloging-in-Publication Data
Lezine, DeQuincy A., 1977–
Eight stories up : an adolescent chooses hope over suicide / DeQuincy A. Lezine,
with David Brent.
p. cm.—(Adolescent mental health initiative)
Includes bibliographical references and index.
ISBN 978-0-19-532556-0—ISBN 978-0-19-532557-7 (pbk)
1. Lezine, DeQuincy A., 1977—Mental health.   2. Teenagers—Suicidal behavior—
Prevention.   I. Brent, David A.   II. Title.
RJ506.S9L49   2008
618.92'858445—dc22   2007047152

9 8 7 6 5 4 3 2
Printed in the United States of America
on acid-free paper

For my wife and partner in life, Myra,
and in memory of my friend, MaryAlice.

Letter to the Reader in Crisis

Dear Reader,

If I were in your position, I would find it hard to believe that somebody I didn't know would really want to talk to me. Yet I really do. I wish I knew your name so that I could make this letter more personal. I wish I could be there with you right now so that you could see the sincerity in my eyes as I listened to you explain your pain to me. I can't. I can only hope that you will read the following words and know that they are written from my heart.

I know that to feel suicidal is to feel unbearable suffering. It hurts so badly that sometimes we just want to cry. Go ahead. I grew up believing that I should never cry, but in fact tears are natural. If you have to cry alone for now, then find a place where you can let those tears go. If it helps to have a friend with you, then give that friend a call or send an e-mail or a text message.

When people are in great pain, it is sometimes hard for them to think about anything other than ending that pain. I remember accidentally getting my finger jammed in my school locker when I was 13. It took everything I had to remember my locker combination so I could get my finger out, all the while distracted by the agony radiating from my hand. I suppose I could have yanked my finger out from the locked door, but that would have made things worse—lacerating the skin or perhaps losing part of the finger altogether. The urge to get rid of suffering is so powerful that we start to consider extreme and permanent solutions for pain relief, when other options are available. It is hard to think clearly when we're in pain—that's why it's not the best time (in fact, it's the worst time) to do something rash, whether yanking a finger out of a locked door or, in the grip of horrific mental pain, considering suicide. How about another analogy? Have you ever stubbed your toe before? When I stub my toe, I end up hopping on one foot and cursing like it's going out of style. Still, I wouldn't be ready to amputate the toe. Yet when it hurt just to be alive, I was ready to cut off living. I was ready to die. But I was wrong to think that dying was the best way to end my pain.

When we have to make a major decision, whether it's to undergo surgery like an amputation, to buy a car, to pick the right college, or to find a good job, most of the time we get help. We get a second opinion. Contemplating suicide is truly a matter of life or death, and your life is more important than cars or jobs or colleges. Doesn't it make sense to get a second opinion about the decision to stop living? Please call some-body—a parent, an older brother or sister, a good friend. You can also call the National Suicide Prevention Lifeline at 1-800-273-TALK (8255),

You can also call the National Suicide Prevention Lifeline at 1-800-273-TALK (8255)

where people are waiting to listen to you and to help you. You are worth the time it takes to get a second opinion about ending your life.

Ultimately, this is a book about options. Suicide is only one of the options for ending your pain, but there are others that are less violent and less permanent. Nobody else can decide for you which options are best. Only you can decide that for yourself. But I think you owe it to yourself to try out some of those other options before you try to kill yourself. You don't know what the future holds, but you rob yourself of the chance to find out what your life can be if you choose to end it now. There is still time for you to find a life worth living. Please don't give up.

Now I'm going to ask you to go make those calls. It takes a lot of strength to ask for help, but I know that you can do it. I'll be here for you when you get back, and we can take a look at some of those options I was talking about.

With every hope for your future,
DeQuincy Lezine

Contents

Foreword

The Adolescent Mental Health Initiative (AMHI) was created by The Annenberg Foundation Trust at Sunnylands to share with mental health professionals, parents, and adolescents the advances in treatment and prevention now available to adolescents with mental health disorders. The Initiative was made possible by the generosity and vision of Ambassadors Walter and Leonore Annenberg, and the project was administered through the Annenberg Public Policy Center of the University of Pennsylvania in partnership with Oxford University Press.

The Initiative began in 2003 with the convening, in Philadelphia and New York, of seven scholarly commissions made up of over 150 leading psychiatrists and psychologists from around the country. Chaired by Drs. Edna B. Foa, Dwight L. Evans, B. Timothy Walsh, Martin E. P. Seligman, Raquel E. Gur, Charles P. O'Brien, and Herbert Hendin, these commissions were tasked with assessing the state of scientific research on the prevalent mental disorders whose onset occurs predominantly between the ages of 10 and 22. Their collective findings now appear in a book for mental health professionals and policy makers titled *Treating and Preventing Adolescent Mental Health Disorders* (2005). As the first product of the Initiative, that book also identified a research agenda that would best advance our ability to prevent and treat these disorders, among them anxiety disorders, depression and bi-polar disorder, eating disorders, substance abuse, and schizo-phrenia.

The second prong of the Initiative's three-part effort is a series of smaller books for general readers. Some of the books are designed primarily for parents of adolescents with a specific mental health disorder. And some, including this one, are aimed at adolescents themselves who are struggling with a mental illness. All of the books draw their scientific information in part from the AMHI professional volume, presenting it in a manner that is accessible to general readers of different ages. The "teen books" also feature the real-life story of one young person who has struggled with—and now manages—a given mental illness. They serve as both a source of solid research about the illness and as a roadmap to recovery for afflicted young people. Thus they offer a unique combination of medical science and firsthand practical wisdom in an effort to inspire adolescents to take an active role in their own recovery.

The third part of the Sunnylands Adolescent Mental Health Initiative consists of two Web sites. The first, www.CopeCareDeal.org, addresses teens. The second, www.oup.com/us/teenmentalhealth, provides updates to the medical community on matters discussed in *Treating and Preventing Adolescent Mental Health Disorders,* the AMHI professional book.

We hope that you find this volume, as one of the fruits of the Initiative, to be helpful and enlightening.

Patrick Jamieson, Ph.D.
Series Editor
Adolescent Risk Communication Institute
Annenberg Public Policy Center
University of Pennsylvania
Philadelphia, PA

Preface

A lexander!" I heard my father's voice roaring across the lake and careening through the valleys. My friend and I had gone exploring. Two fairly typical teenage boys, we had found a small tract of land on the opposite side of the lake from where our families had anchored the houseboat we were vacationing in. In uncharted territory, there were no signs of a human presence over here, and helping my friend out of a small patch of quicksand heightened the thrill of the adventure. I fancied myself an explorer. My father, on the other hand, probably thought I was a heart attack waiting to happen. "Alexander!" We dashed back to the inflatable raft and paddled back toward the group, as if our speed could lessen the wrath that was sure to follow. It was always my nature to push the boundaries.

My father gave me the name Alexander. It is my middle name, the one he used when I had ventured too far or touched some new nerve. Sometimes he would yell it when I had disappeared beyond the limits of where he could see. Other times, he would say it quietly, usually twice, while shaking his head, as if "Alexander . . . Alexander" meant, "What am I going to do with you, boy?"

Generally, people tend to drop their middle names or use just a single initial between their first and last names, but mine seemed to reflect my essential nature, and my future career. My father named me after Alexander the Great, the undefeated Greek military commander, foreshadowing a lifetime of battles and victories. The name originates from the roots *alexis* (refuge, protection, defense) and *andros* (man), thus Alexander is a "protector or defender of man." True to both meanings of my name, I fight to protect those who have no other guardian.

I am, in short, an advocate.

An advocate speaks or acts on behalf of others, prompted by a sense of social justice, human rights, or moral values. In some ways, advocates are idealists. Undeterred by finding an imperfect reality, the advocate tries to make the world a better place.

My personality and life experiences seem to have prepared me for an advocacy role. My childhood wasn't easy. I grew up on the fringes of various social groups within the Los Angeles school system. I was bullied by some of my peers, and in general I stood apart from my world, never quite settling into the center of the cliques of athletes, artists, or academics in the schools I attended, even though I was athletic, artistic, and academically inclined myself. In hindsight, I realize that empathy connected the dots, linking me to diverse peer groups and earning me a large but shallow social network, with only a few close friends. With empathy I could understand many different kinds of people, and I often lived vicariously through them. I agonized when friends and family were impoverished, imprisoned, bankrupted, discriminated against, fired from jobs, raped, addicted, and brutally murdered. I tasted desperation when they joined gangs, prostituted, gambled, and sold drugs. But I also rejoiced in their redemption as they finished rehab, sobered up, supported families, taught themselves to read, and earned college scholarships. This mixture of pain and pride in the hardships and triumphs of others—this mixture of agony and joy for those around me—has formed the foundation for my advocacy as much as my own personal experiences have. For me, advocacy is based on empathy for what others are going through, and a passion for making things better.

Why an Advocate for Suicide Prevention

Suicide can lurk just beneath the surface of many tragic and painful emotional experiences in life. There are myriad paths that may take a person perilously close to self-destruction. What advocacy cause is more important than the struggle between life and death? And yet the twin stigmas associated with mental illness and death can complicate this struggle: Many people don't understand mental illness, and so try to distance themselves from it. Likewise, people fear death, as if it were somehow contagious, and may hesitate to talk about it. This combination has thwarted many of the most ardent suicide prevention and mental health advocates, and can make anyone's personal struggle against suicide even more difficult and isolating.

Suicide prevention is, in other words, a formidable challenge. Some say it is impossible for our society to win the fight against suicide. Hence my self-selected nickname, Quix, from Don Quixote de la Mancha, the tragic hero of Cervantes's novel *Don Quixote.* You see, I, too, am pursuing a so-called impossible dream: eradicating youth suicide from our society. Yet I didn't pick this fight with suicide. It chose me.

In the middle of my first semester in college on the East Coast, relentless thoughts of suicide caught me with my guard down. With one swift kick in the ass, I was knocked flat, and the specter of suicide towered over me. I thought about death constantly, engaged in ever riskier activities, and planned my final moments with the kind of methodical care that a demolition crew puts into razing a building. Fortunately for me, my plans were disrupted. I found myself hospitalized, and suddenly I was one of those neglected mentally ill—in my case, a forsaken suicidal youth with, eventually, a diagnosis of bipolar disorder. Only then did I notice that there were many other people suffering from psychological injuries, many others who, like me, lived daily with the threat of a self-inflicted death. I saw that there were other young adults in the psychiatric hospital besides myself. Before, I had ignored these kinds of people. I thought they were *crazy,* and while I had sympathy for them, I had no empathy as yet—their pain had been too foreign to me. I suppose I had to get knocked down myself by the suicidal urge for that to change. On the ward, I met a middle-aged man with depression who had tried all of the available antidepressant medications, as well as electroconvulsive therapy, without success. Still, he had not given up hope of recovery. I could not walk away from my own brush with suicide and forget about that man or his hope, or forget about the many others who battled the same demons; this is the curse and the blessing of empathy.

When I was released from the psychiatric hospital, two thoughts occurred to me: First, things shouldn't have to go to this extreme for someone to get help—why was it that I hadn't gotten meaningful help long before I became suicidal? Second, what can I do to stop others from having to experience this type of suffering? My pain became my passion as I decided to dedicate my life and career to promoting mental health and preventing youth suicide. Through college, graduate school, and postdoctoral training, I studied suicide. I have since worked with suicidal youth in peer support groups, as a therapist and as a friend. I have known what it's like to live with suicidal family members, and to date someone who became suicidal. I have suffered the grief of friends' suicides in my private life, and lost a client to suicide in my professional life. Meanwhile, I have advocated publicly for suicide prevention at the college, state, and national level.

How This Book Came To Be

The general idea for this book was born in 2003, when seven scholarly commissions on adolescent mental health were convened by the Annenberg Foundation Trust at Sunnylands. The psychiatrists and psychologists on these commissions were charged with examining the state of the science on mental disorders that strike teenagers and young adults, and youth suicide was among the topics studied. Several books on, or drawing from, the findings of these commissions followed, including the one you hold in your hands.

David Brent, M.D., was a member of the commission on youth suicide prevention, and he is also the medical adviser for this book. Dr. Brent is Academic Chief of Child and Adolescent Psychiatry at the prestigious Western Psychiatric Institute and Clinic, and Professor of Psychiatry, Pediatrics, and Epidemiology at the University of Pittsburgh School of Medicine. For many years, he has studied and treated young people who are at risk for suicide, so he brings a wealth of experience and wisdom to these pages.

This book also came to be for another reason. I spent a lot of time feeling lost and helpless when I was suicidal. Desperate to make sense of everything that was happening, I rummaged through the campus libraries, seeking wisdom from the many books on suicide but often leaving dissatisfied. Simply put, something was missing. I found no book that explained what I was going through, or that helped to ease my suffering in an empathetic, understanding way. I yearned for the voice of an author who had lived through the suicidal nightmare and recovered—not just some academic in an ivory tower who studied charts and statistics. I didn't need someone else to tell me that "everything is going to be all right," someone who would smile tentatively, go home, and forget about me. I needed someone who would honestly say, "Hell, yeah, it's dark out there, but I'm going to stay with you till we see daylight." Here is that book. As I write these words, just knowing that you're reading them encourages me to write on. And as you read, I will be there with you. Perhaps if this book is helpful to you and other readers, my suffering will not have been in vain.

And so, ultimately, this book is meant to be two things. First, it is intended as a personal guide, a hopeful light to help you get through the suicidal darkness. When we are lost, we look for a guide who can help lead us to our destination. (Of course, the guide can't tell you where you *want* to go—that's your job. You didn't think I was going to do all the work, right?) In a guide, we seek the knowledge of a trustworthy and experienced traveler, and I humbly suggest that I can play that role for you. I'm in a unique position to guide you through your suicidal crisis, as I've been there myself and have since made suicide prevention my career. Through telling you about my own experiences in this book, I hope to be able to help lead you out of your crisis and to arm you with support in getting help and staying healthy.

Second, this book should be a resource that you can look to for answers to the how's and why's of suicide. With Dr. Brent's help, I've packed into this book the information you need—about what kinds of circumstances and situations might make a person more likely to feel suicidal, what kinds of treatments are available to you, how to make the most of those treatments, and much more. I've drawn both on my personal experience and on scientific evidence as I talk about how I found a life worth living and about how you can, too. This way, I hope you will see that a person *can* survive a suicidal crisis and that I'm not the only one who has done so.

You've probably noticed that I have used the word *hope* a lot in the past several pages. That in essence is what this book is about, and in the following pages, I will try to convey to you what the word really means and to give you *realistic hope* for your own future. The suicidal urge tricks us into feeling as if all hope is incinerated, leaving only ashes in its wake. My aim for this book is to show that these feelings, however real they may seem, aren't the whole truth. How suicidal thinking *feels* and what is objectively *true* are very different. If you know someone who has endured these thoughts, or if you are that someone, then this book is for you. We can get past the pain; we can find new hope.

Make no mistake: It takes courage to work on recovery, and courage to discuss the personal side of suicide. After all, nobody ponders death because of trivial matters. Although some people may feel suicidal despite the absence of a traumatic past, facing their personal demons will still be difficult for them. For others, it will be even more so. Sometimes divulging our suicidal thoughts may mean revealing hidden family secrets, or scars of childhood, or the heavy burden of mental illness. Exploring how our suicidal crisis developed may mean digging up dormant agonies, or laying bare the most intimate and painful memories. Many people may even feel ashamed to discuss their suicidal urges.

Ever since I made public my struggle with suicide, through books and the media, I've felt anxious about how family and friends will react when they come across themselves in my story. In fact, in this book, I have changed or avoided mentioning the names of several people in an effort to protect their privacy. The story nevertheless is public record now, and I have told it here and elsewhere as openly as I can, despite my worry about the potential retaliation or stigma that could follow public disclosure of my suicidal past. Why? Because I have a fear that is greater than these anxieties about disclosure: my fear of losing you, the reader, to a suicidal death. I know that I cannot presume to walk beside you on your journey through the darkness unless I am honest with you about my own dark times. Otherwise, it would sound hollow for me to say that I empathize. I am willing to take the risk of revealing my struggles, so that you might believe in the reasons for hope. You are worth it.

Can You Trust Me?

Maybe I'm a cynic, but I doubt I'm the only person who wonders what authors have to gain by writing or selling a book. For the record, I received only modest compensation for my time in writing *Eight Stories Up*. I did not create any of the therapies, medications, or programs that this book describes, and I receive no profits or kickbacks on any of them. I don't own any stocks in pharmaceutical companies. In short, I have nothing to gain by advising you to try a particular type of therapy, consider a certain medication, or think about a certain option. My only aim in writing this book is to help you find the alternatives that people (including me) are pursuing to overcome their suffering without dying.

And indeed, I am writing directly to *you*, the teen or young adult who has thought about or attempted suicide. While

I welcome our invited guests who also read this book so that they can assist us with our recovery, I am not writing primarily to them. You might be thinking, *Why are you writing to me? You don't even know me.* You're right; of course, I don't know you, or your unique situation. Nevertheless, I do not want you to try (again) to kill yourself. I am advocating for your *right* to have a good life. I know that you're worth fighting for.

I don't expect you to trust me right from the start; I wouldn't if I were you. I only ask that you give me the chance to earn your trust. Usually, authors ask for trust based on their credentials, their name recognition, or their ability to cite research evidence to back up their arguments. Sure, those things are important, and between Dr. Brent and me, you will have all of that. Still, I think you deserve more than that because, well, this is *your life* we're talking about here. I hope you'll find you can trust me because I won't bullshit you. I know that if you find honesty and sincerity in these pages, then you might believe that the reasons for hope are real.

Eight Stories Up

Chapter One

Crisis

Y ou're about to read the journal entry I wrote right after my
first brush with suicide in college. I wrote it in a hardcover
journal that I had received as a going-away gift just before
freshman year. As I look at it now, I realize the irony of the
cover art: It is from the inside of an Egyptian coffin and depicts
Anubis, the jackal-headed guardian of the dead.

Walking Into Madness

October 2, 1995, 4:00 A.M.

I think I flipped today. . . . I talked to Mom on the phone and
that question, "How do you feel?," came up again. How do
I feel? Does she really want to know? Frustrated but goal-
driven, hopeless yet motivated, alone with friends, lost but in
the middle of it all, like I've lost all faith, yet stronger than I've
ever been.

"How do you feel?" What kind of question is that? I feel like
a million and 15 different people live in my head, like I'm
doing all I ever wanted and it's not what I expected, like I'm
not sure whether I can succeed—resentment, envy, despair,

1

hurt, unloved, uncared for, unfound, lonely, estranged, angry, left out, forgotten, I don't know, pick one!!!!

...I tried to keep it together. I visited people. I vented a little. I ate chocolate with my good friend, Amanda, who said I looked "so sad—like you just lost a good friend—like a little kid whose puppy died."

It hurt so bad and I didn't know why. I had to try really hard to keep from crying. My [computer] program wouldn't work, I was frustrated, angry, lost, confused, and about to EXPLODE!

I went for a walk and told myself it was scary because I didn't care about much then. I walked, I looked at the ground moving randomly beneath the soles of my shoes. I walked. I came to the hill and left campus, I walked to the bridge....

The water trickled into the canal and the water—oh, the water—it looked so peaceful and the rail so short. "I wonder how long it would take them to find my body. I wonder who would care. It would probably make the news, it would probably even make the news back home...another Ivy League suicide."

Tears streaked from my eyes and burned down my cheeks. Why! Nobody gives a damn and they all love not you, my friend. Fuck them all! The world can go to hell! I laughed and cried. I laughed!? I cracked. I had lost it and I was loving it.

I came to a highway and thought about jumping [off the overpass]. Then I did it. I came around to the fence parallel to the highway. "I know what people are thinking when they try to cross the highway, they're just not fast enough. I am." My inhibitions, common sense, logical thought, and fear would have stopped me, normally. Not tonight.

Eight lanes of freeway, of big rig trucks and late-night commuters, eight lanes I crossed. I didn't get hit, or nicked, or anything. I made it! I screamed. It felt good.

A Colossal Wave of Despair

Normally I tell people that you don't just wake up one day and say, "Hey, I'm suicidal today." No one moment, no single event, is enough by itself to create a suicidal crisis. Instead, multiple events or situations, known as *risk factors,* combine to increase the chances that a

You don't just wake up one day and say, "Hey, I'm suicidal today."

person will consider and attempt suicide. But one of the paradoxes of suicide is that sometimes it can *seem* as though it happens for a single reason. Sometimes bad things seem to happen all at once, and as the risk factors pile up, there is a moment when a person's mental state suddenly crosses a certain threshold and the scales tilt in favor of death. I've always thought of my suicidal crisis as a tsunami. The colossal wave probably started as a tiny ripple somewhere miles off the coast, but that didn't really matter during the awful moment when the sea came rushing in, engulfing my world. When my suicidal crisis finally hit, I realized that I could not outrun it and I could not hide from it, and that terrified me.

It was October 1st, and I was in my freshman year at college. On that night, I crossed the line from being a person "at risk for suicide" to one who was "suicidal." Before that, I had made a practice of not thinking about stressful circumstances. I numbed out. There were so many feelings and memories from my childhood, both bad and good, that I had swept under my mental rug. I had squished them into a jar. I guess it was inevitable that the jar would eventually break. When it did break that night, all of the painful emotions of my past rushed in to torment me; everything came barreling down on me at once. I didn't have the words to describe all these feelings at the time. Instead, I called them all *anger.* That was just a convenient label, a stereotypical male emotional response. My emotional pain was built on more than rage alone. I was also experiencing an unhealthy onslaught of disappointment, anxiety, and shame.

For starters, I felt alone. I was afraid that I would never fit in with a group of peers, that the peer rejection of my childhood would revisit me constantly—that I'd always feel that I didn't belong. I told you earlier that I "grew up on the fringes" socially and that I benefited from that experience. But at the time, I didn't see it that way. Instead, I felt like an outcast as a child—hurt, lonely, abandoned. I felt the same way in college and worried about not being able to cut it. Just a poor kid from inner-city Los Angeles, I'd been accepted to a prestigious Ivy League university where my classmates were the valedictorians, *magna cum laudes,* and "with honors" crowd. Even with good grades, I felt like a pathetic failure, absolutely worthless. The sheer weight of this inexplicable despair crushed my soul, burdening me with heartache, misery, and anguish. I couldn't figure it all out, and that frustrated me—I prided myself on being able to figure things out. How could I be so confused?

I couldn't think straight. Strange yet familiar thoughts were whipping through my mind.

I can't take this shit anymore . . .
I don't want to live anymore . . .
Death is the only way out . . .
I want to die . . .

Of course, I kept all of this to myself as much as possible—in the beginning, at least. I faked the smiles and laughs, trying my best to look like what I thought college students were supposed to look like.

The college years were supposed to be the best years of my life. I was supposed to reward my family for the sacrifices they'd made to send me to college, and become a role model for the kids back at home. Everybody had looked so proud when they'd sent me off. I couldn't let everybody down. And anyhow, what would people think about me if I told them about my thoughts and feelings? I know what *I* would have thought, had I been in their shoes: I would have thought, *This guy is crazy.* What could be worse than that? This line of thinking amplified the loneliness. Not only did I feel terrible, but I was convinced no one could ever possibly empathize with the pain I was feeling. *Nobody can understand this,* I thought. *They will all think that I have lost my mind.* I was certain that I was alone in thinking about suicide.

Death on the Mind

Death had branded me. It was as if it had taken a blazing firebrand and scorched its dark mark into the base of my skull. At first, I believed the suicidal thoughts were a passing phase, something that I would wake up from or be able to shake off. But I soon found that the idea of dying just wouldn't go away. The suicidal urge became a constant and unwanted companion, slowly but surely wearing down my will to live. Death sounded peaceful, like a welcome relief. I

At first, I believed the suicidal thoughts were a passing phase, something that I would wake up from or be able to shake off. But I soon found that the idea of dying just wouldn't go away.

idealized it and put it up on a pedestal. I just wanted all the pain of living, all of those negative emotions, negative thoughts, and negative experiences, to cease and desist.

On the worst days, my thoughts as I walked to class would go something like this:

I stop to cross the street. I see a police officer helping to direct traffic. What if he shot me? Oh yeah. Security officers at the university don't carry sidearms. What if I got hit by a car, or maybe that tan minivan? The red hand of the crossing signal disappears, replaced by a little white walking man and a "chirp chirp" that says that for now I am safe to cross the street. Closing my eyes, I step off the curb, imagining that I am stepping off a building, but the fall is short. I look around, wondering if anybody noticed me. Of course not, they are all too busy being happy. Happy? What does that feel like? Shit. I can't even remember. I pass a tree and think about hanging. I muse that the tree is probably taunting me, saying, "My branches will break before I let you hang from me, you freak." The thought lingers as I enter class and attempt to concentrate on the lecture. It is difficult. Thoughts of suicide try to crowd out the course material. Come on, Quix. Concentrate, dammit. Focus. But death sounds so good.

Warning Signs for Suicide

You might wonder what signs indicate that a person may be considering suicide. Here are some that suicide prevention experts seem to agree on. The person is

- Experiencing dramatic mood changes (e.g., increased turbulence vs. sudden calm)

(continued)

- Expressing anger and rage
- Feeling anxiety or agitation
- Having a lack of purpose in life or no reason for living
- Feeling trapped
- Withdrawing from friends and family
- Feeling hopeless
- Abusing substances, including alcohol, illegal drugs, and prescription medications
- Engaging in reckless behavior
- Talking or thinking about suicide

Even without a degree in psychology, I knew that this was a bad sign. I looked up information on the Internet and found the Web site for a group called Suicide Awareness Voices for Education (SAVE). They listed suicide "warning signs," thoughts and behaviors that indicate suicidal danger, including frequent *suicidal ideation* (the term that mental health professionals use to describe thoughts about suicide). This new information left me feeling like I wasn't so alone—others had developed the same patterns. Yet I was despondent when I recognized the danger I was in.

The Jump

I couldn't shake the explosive cocktail of depression and rage from the night that I snapped and intentionally risked my life by running across a busy highway. More and more, over the next several weeks, my thoughts turned to suicide. In many scenarios that I imagined, I would die in a way that would make other people "sorry for screwing up my life." I loved my family and friends, but I also wanted them to understand the depth of my pain. Killing myself would surely tell them just how deep it was. I even fantasized about going out in some kind of a blaze of glory, and started collecting materials for a firebomb. They sat in my closet unassembled, and when a friend asked about them, I said they were for a physics project, then got rid of everything. I guess I was ambivalent. Suicide sounded so good, but part of me really did not want to go that route. I wanted things to work out, I wanted to live, but I did not want to live with that kind of pain anymore. And in fact, nearly everyone who considers suicide has this same internal struggle between the desire to live and the desire to die. Our goal must be to tip the scales in favor of life: Solve the problems we're facing (decrease the reasons for dying), and live a happy and meaningful life (increase the reasons for living).

I wanted to live, but I did not want to live with that kind of pain anymore.

Looking back, I wonder if I would still be here if I had been drinking alcohol when I was so desperate; alcohol use, as we'll see, increases the odds that a person will impulsively take his or her own life. Would things have been different if I had had a gun, which would have made the possibility of suicide so much more immediate? As painful as that is to think about, far too many young people make a single—and deadly—suicide attempt when they have ready access to such lethal means.

Anyhow, I silently tried to kill myself over the following two months. I didn't tell anyone about the full extent of my suicidal despair, not until the end of November. I was always a quiet thinker, considering many different aspects of a problem before taking action, and not always saying what was going through my mind. (That always used to get on my math teachers' nerves: "Show your work," they'd say, even though I had the right answer.) Why should planning my own death have been any different? I couldn't tell people about everything I was thinking about doing—they would have thought I was crazy.

Initially, I tried passive ways to die. I would lie across the train tracks, listening to music and hoping to be run down by the next commuter rail. The train never came. *Damn train.* Then I started wandering the streets at night, in the bad neighborhoods I wasn't supposed to go to. My dad had always said not to do that because it was dangerous. I was looking for a mugger who would demand my wallet. I would laugh and maybe push him a little, then a little more, until he'd just get pissed off and shoot me. But I encountered no muggers—just a few possibilities who crossed to the other side of the street as I passed. Maybe all the criminals had decided to move somewhere else. Maybe they chose to seek quarry other than a six-foot-five man with nothing to lose. *Cowards,* I thought.

One night, I was out at about two in the morning looking for trouble, when the heavens opened up and started raining on me. The sudden sprinkle rapidly progressed to a torrential downpour. *Who would keep walking in this weather except crazy people?* I asked myself. I fell to my knees, crying for the loss of who I was and troubled by who I had become. The smell of wet asphalt filled my lungs as the huge drops pounded on my limp figure, and I began to pray:

Why, God, why am I still here? I ask for the best for my family and friends, as always. Tonight, I do not ask for riches, or health, or love, or longevity. No, God. Tonight, I ask only one thing. Please let me die. I hurt so bad. I can't take this anymore. Please let me die. Amen.

Apparently, I would get no help from above in this endeavor, for nothing happened and I did not die that night. *Fine.* I tried to remember the suicides I had seen on television or read about somewhere. People shoot themselves. There weren't many gun shops near campus, but there was a pawn shop that looked promising. I stopped to think about what might happen. A black adolescent walks into a pawn shop to buy a handgun. I couldn't tell the pawnbroker that I wanted it for shooting myself. He would call the police for sure. Then they'd call the men in white coats to take me away. Besides, guns were expensive. I then tried to make my own gun, but that proved to be much harder than I expected.

My thoughts turned to cutting my wrists or hanging myself, but those seemed like rather painful and uncertain ways to die. In fact, I did try cutting myself, and it just hurt like hell. When I thought about hanging myself, I figured that with my luck my neck wouldn't break, and I'd just swing there slowly choking to death. My roommate or best friend would have to come and identify my body after I had soiled my pants and my reputation. That was clearly not the way to go.

Eventually, I settled on "the jump" as my method of choice. There were practical reasons for this choice. Jumping had a fairly high lethality rate, according to the information I had. Unlike buying a gun or having a length of rope hanging out in my dorm room, making preparations to jump off a tall building could be done without arousing suspicion. But there were other reasons that jumping resonated with me. I simply liked the idea. Jumping seemed peaceful, like flying or gliding to my death, and yet dramatic—fitting for someone with an artistic temperament. I wanted to end like all the comic book characters I had created over the years. I pictured myself as something of a tragic hero, and heroes have only spectacular deaths. Jumping was it for me. It also had an athletic touch: In basketball, I was known on the playground for my turn-around jump shot, and so this plan would be reminiscent of that reputation—just one last jump. For those of us who get attached to a particular method of suicide, I guess there is always some special significance.

Everything had to be just right. The act had to have elements of careful planning, adventure, and intrigue. It had to have symbolism and drama. The buildings downtown were promising because of their height. A number of them were hotels, so there would be relatively easy access even at night. I scoped out several hotels, one with twenty stories, another with even more, until I settled on one hotel in particular: one connected to an eight-story parking garage. On a reconnaissance run, I figured out what I needed to gain access to the roof of the hotel, or at least the garage, and secured the tools from a local hardware store. Everything went into a black backpack. I chose an outfit of black and blue (to symbolize my bruised soul), and business casual to decrease suspicion. I could easily walk through the front door of a hotel in a shirt and tie—it would be much harder wearing a black hoodie.

Saying Goodbye

The peak of my suicidal crisis was in late November 1995. I had been corresponding with Toni, a good friend back in Los Angeles. During high school we were in the same religious congregation and were roughly the same age. I thought that perhaps there was a mutual romantic attraction between us. I already thought I didn't have too much to lose, so I asked her if she felt the same way about me that I felt about her. In hindsight, the situation was difficult and awkward for far too many reasons (differing cultural beliefs around dating, the long distance between us, and, of course, my recent depressive suicidal crisis). I put Toni in a tough spot, and she wanted to "just be friends." After that, I felt like I had been rejected one too many times. Within a few days I had finalized plans, picked the date of the jump (December 1), written a suicide note, and started distancing myself from Toni, my high school friends, and my best friend at college, Amanda. I wrote e-mails trying to explain to those close to me why I felt I had to die. I can't think of a better way to describe the confusing emotional rollercoaster that my friends and I went through in that short time than to quote from some of those messages.

I wrote e-mails trying to explain to those close to me why I felt I had to die.

4:41 A.M.

I'm telling you this has been The Hardest time of my life. . . . Do you know what I went to do tonight? I went to scope out buildings just in case . . . pretty scary, huh? Pretty damn cold, too. . . . I should have done that while the sun was still up. Anyhow, I wanted to have a definite plan just in case . . . by the time I got back I wasn't sure exactly why I wanted a "just in case" plan, but I'm still trying to figure out a lot of that suicidal stuff anyway. . . . I had a definite plan at that time. I would try to get into one building that would allow me at least 20 stories. Then again, I had a couple of other options that would allow me to get even higher.

4:50 A.M.

As hard as it is to get up each morning and tell myself, "I'm going to live another day," and NOT break down and cry because I'm still alive . . . I am not planning on giving up, although I did lay out a very precise plan for my self-termination, including where and how I could go . . . from eight stories up . . . which means I am still a high-risk suicidal.

I had to stop myself from jumping today . . . I don't know what it was, but something grabbed me and had me go out for a walk in the FREEZING cold and scope out the possibilities for a jump. I found one! As I was standing on the eighth-story top of the parking garage connected to the hotel, I looked over and I thought, "Scary. I could never . . . " but I didn't get finished because I could feel myself leaning forward, and I had to pull back . . . thank God, I did . . . and walked back down.

I'm back on the edge right now, but not so close to the end of it to be thinking about jumping. I'm just kind of sitting there, I guess . . . It's like I was about to hop and head back down (ha . . .) and I've been injured quite a bit within the last days and I've been given a bit to hope for at the same time . . . it's screwing up my head. . . . I can't think clearly. . . .

I am exhausted mentally, emotionally, and physically, grasping at straws . . . losing my mind perhaps?

I'd better go. Anyhow, just wanted to let you know that I am getting better. It is a very slow process, but I am . . . still in a lot of pain, though . . . funny thing is I haven't felt so good in a long time as I did earlier this week, but I still have the symptoms of a high-risk suicidal. . . . I suppose it is a lot deeper rooted than I had counted on. . . .

1:51 P.M.

I hope I haven't stressed you too much, I'm so sorry about that. Been in a different state of mind. Things aren't clear right now, nothing is rational . . . feels like I'm fading out . . . I'm losing it. . . .

Gotta go . . . don't feel well . . . not sick . . . not depressed really . . . not angry . . . not sad . . . not lonely . . . not even empty really . . . not in pain . . . I'm not sure what it is . . . of course, it's not happiness . . . not joy . . . not optimism . . .

nothing good like that either. I don't know what it is, it's kind of a void feeling. It's strange.

I won't ever see 19. It's a good time to die. I know that I need to end the pain . . . that's all I need to know. I know the lethality rate for buildings 6 stories and that it increases after that.

7:04 P.M.

I have redefined my current state. I am dead. That is why there are no feelings, why I can't feel my heart beating, why it feels like I have to TRY just to breathe another breath of air. . . . You probably should have given up while you had the chance to do so. Give up on me. Please? For your sake. . . . I am a sinking ship, leave me while you are still able to. Leave me to die alone . . . please? I want to remember you the way you were tonight . . . happy. When I am on top of that roof, standing there . . . I will be happy as well.

How serious am I? I have a suicide note drafted and carefully placed in an envelope, I have a specific plan of action and a fall-back plan. I know the lethality of my actions, and I know the place where I can do so successfully.

You've got to be careful . . . right now there is a battle going on in my mind. . . . Part of me, what is left of that rational Quix, the psychologist, is saying, "You've at least got to warn them," . . . he knows I'm reaching out . . . that there is probably some part of my stupid subconscious that wants to live . . . it is battling with my conscious, which has thought of nothing but suicide for the past two weeks or so and is set on the deed. . . .

I suppose in a way . . . that part that is getting smaller by the moment is saying "HELP!!!!!!!" And the other part is trying to shut him up. . . . I suppose I could continue life if I tried, but you know what? I couldn't even find a reason to try any longer. . . .

Woke up this morning . . . felt like I had a hole in my chest. Felt like I haven't slept in years, but I've been getting more than enough sleep. Felt like I didn't have any feeling in my body . . . only reason I ate was because it seemed like something I usually did around that time. . . . Haven't been hungry . . . haven't been thirsty . . . no pain . . . no more. . . . I can't take the pain anymore . . . I just can't do it.

I am in a very dangerous and deadly situation right now . . . don't know what else to say or do . . . done all I could. Tried harder than I even thought possible. Scars I thought had healed a long time ago were reopened within the last couple of weeks . . . wounds I thought I had set aside have come back to haunt me . . . pains I thought I had gotten over returned . . . and within the last two months I have had more to deal with *. . . wounds I thought I had set aside have come back to haunt me . . . pains I thought I had gotten over returned . . .* than I have during my entire life . . . 18 years of suffering brought to a painful realization in the midst of depression and confusion in a new environment was enough to set me down the path I had been set up for these past 10–11 years. . . . that's how long it's been building up . . . like a volcano or quake. . . .

Gotta go now. . . .

As I hit "send" on that message, I felt a hand on my shoulder. I turned to see two university police officers, accompanied by two of my unit counselors (RAs). They had come to the computer lab to escort me out. My friends hadn't just been reading and replying to all those e-mails—they had been trying to keep me online. They were also contacting each other and setting up a Save Quix Network. They had called the university and initiated the intervention. I had had a serious intent to die that week, so I guess my friends saved my life.

One of Many in a Desolate Club

Obviously, I am just one individual among many who have come to know the agony of the suicidal urge. I realized, over time, that I was part of a much larger and incredibly diverse group of people—perhaps you are an unlucky member of our club, too. Researchers have conducted numerous studies in an attempt to find out how many people belong to this club, but it's not an exact science. Thanks to surveys completed by hundreds of young people, though, we do have at least a sense of how often suicide or suicidal thinking strikes in our communities; mental health researchers use these numbers to try and tease out the relationships between suicide and different groups of people, and to learn how best to go about preventing suicide and treating suicidal people.

How Many Think about Suicide?

Research has shown that at least 1 out of every 10 people aged 15 to 24 in the United States has thought about suicide (i.e., has had suicidal ideation). The numbers are probably much lower than they are in reality, though, because young people who are not in school (the most likely place they'd complete a survey) are more likely to think about or attempt suicide.

Where do the numbers come from? Every two years, the Centers for Disease Control and Prevention (CDC), as part of its Youth Risk Behavior Survey (YRBS), ask a sample of high school students (grades 9–12) from across the United States if they "seriously considered attempting suicide during the past 12 months." In 2005, 17% of students said they had had suicidal thoughts (22% of females, 12% of males). In a separate national survey that has followed a group of adolescents for years, 16% of youth in grades 7 through 12 had seriously considered suicide during the past year. The CDC has asked college students about suicidal thoughts only once (in 1995), and 11% of students ages 18 to 24 reported having such suicidal thoughts. The American College Health Association (ACHA) has asked college students that question since 2000 on the National College Health Assessment, and 10% to 11% of students consistently report having had suicidal thoughts in the past year.

How Many Act on the Suicidal Urge?

Scientists have drawn a distinction between people who think about suicide and those who have actually tried to harm themselves. It is this latter group, a much smaller proportion of people, that we need to worry about the most. The national surveys just mentioned have also polled adolescents and young adults in the United States on actual suicide attempts. In the 2005 YRBS, 13% of high school students said that they had made a plan about how they would attempt suicide during the previous year. Eight percent attempted suicide at least once, and 2% said that they had made a suicide attempt that was dangerous enough to require medical treatment. The other national survey of high school students found that 5% of adolescents had acted on their suicidal thoughts by making at least one suicide attempt. In the 1995 CDC survey of college students 18 to 24 years old, 8% said that they had a suicide plan, 2% attempted suicide at least once, and 0.4% (4 out of 1,000) reported an attempt that needed medical attention. In the 2006 ACHA survey, 1% of college students said that they had attempted suicide during the past year.

What Qualifies as a Suicide Attempt?

You may be wondering where dangerous behavior ends and suicide attempts begin. Is driving too fast a suicide attempt? What if it's dark out, and the road is slippery? Or if the car's headlights are turned off? Where do we draw the line? There is no easy way to answer these questions, and mental health professionals themselves don't always seem to agree. Part of the problem is that researchers just can't get into the heads of people who are experiencing suicidal urges—we can only study what they say and what they do. Another problem is with terminology. Terms used to describe suicidal behavior include, among others:

- *Suicide,* the act of killing oneself deliberately.
- *Suicide attempt,* a deliberate attempt to die that nevertheless does not result in death.
- *Parasuicide,* a self-inflicted injury with or without any intent to die (but which sometimes results in death anyway). Also known as *deliberate self-harm.*
- *Suicide gesture,* a self-inflicted injury that looks like a suicide attempt, but the intent is to get something (like attention or love) from someone else.
- *Victim-precipitated homicide,* an act in which someone deliberately provokes another person into using lethal force.

As you can imagine, there is a lot of debate about at least a few of these terms—about where the boundaries should be between them, what kinds of behaviors they should include, and whether they all even qualify as suicidal acts. The bottom line, for us, should be that *any* deliberately harmful act should be taken as a sign that something is very wrong. If you find yourself exhibiting any of these behaviors, *no matter how minor they may seem,* please talk to a mental health professional about them right away.

Young women attempt suicide more often than their male counterparts do. In the 2005 YRBS, 11% of female students had attempted suicide, compared to 6% of male students. The difference is slightly smaller for suicide attempts that need medical attention: 3% of female students and 2% of male students.

How Many Die by Suicide?

Like me, the adolescents and young adults that complete surveys have lived to tell others about their suicide attempts. Not everyone gets that chance. In 2004, for example, we lost 283 young adolescents (10–14 years old), 1,700 teens (15–19 years old), and 2,616 young adults (20–24 years old) to suicide. That's a total of 4,599 people between the ages of 10 and 24 who killed themselves in 2004—imagine 70 school busses full of young people who have decided to drive off a cliff. Preliminary data from the CDC indicate that 4,409 people between the ages of 5 and 24 killed themselves in 2005.

Like me, the adolescents and young adults that complete surveys have lived to tell others about their suicide attempts. Not everyone gets that chance.

In contrast to the higher distribution of females to males who attempt suicide, males die by suicide almost six times as often as females do. This may be because they tend to select more lethal means. Fortunately, suicide is rather rare: 1.3 people per 100,000 for 10- to 14-year-olds; 8.2 per 100,000 for 15- to 19-year-olds; and 12.5 per 100,000 for 20- to 24-year-olds. But while suicide is rare, it is still the third leading cause of death among young people, right after accidents and homicide. (Also, keep in mind that some deaths classified as accidents may really have been suicides.)

Ethnicity and Suicidal Behavior

Research studies on suicidal behavior have been primarily conducted with white participants. Until recently, many reports did not even specify the racial or ethnic identities of people who participated in the study. Regardless of race or ethnicity, people in urban settings, schools or colleges, and hospitals are most likely to get recruited for research studies. People who are not in one of those categories, including members of many minority groups, are not likely to be represented in research. Population differences by region also influence research results. For instance, if most studies are conducted in the Northeast, then any group that is concentrated in the Southwest or other parts of the country will be under-represented.

The data that I am about to present about suicidal behavior among minority groups in the United States are therefore limited in some ways. First of all, the information isn't very specific—statistics on suicide within ethnic minority groups often lump very different subgroups together into larger categories. For example, there are vast cultural differences between peoples of Latin American descent, but many studies consider them to be one homogenous group. You should also keep in mind the following issues that affect the quality of the data we have:

1. Studies show that individuals from racial or ethnic minority groups who have died by suicide are more likely to have been misclassified as "accidental" or "unknown" deaths. We don't know exactly why this is the case, although in part it may be due to differences in the methods that groups use for suicide (such as guns, drug overdose, or drowning). The result is that the number of recorded suicides in ethnic and minority

> The number of recorded suicides in ethnic and minority groups is almost certainly lower than the actual number of suicide deaths.

groups is almost certainly lower than the actual number of suicide deaths.

2. Many racial or ethnic minority groups have extremely negative views of mental illness and mental health care, so many individuals in these groups may not report suicide attempts or seek help from mental health professionals. The result is that we know less about suicidality among these groups than we do about suicidality among groups for whom the issue is less taboo.

AFRICAN AMERICANS

Suicide is the third leading cause of death for 15- to 24-year-old African Americans. The highest suicide rate is among 20- to 24-year old males, but black women are almost twice as likely to attempt suicide compared to black men (9.8% vs. 5.2%). In 2005, compared to the national average, fewer African American high school students seriously considered suicide (12.2% vs. 16.9%) or attempted suicide (7.6% vs. 8.4%). However, recent research indicates that over the lifetime, the number of African Americans who attempt suicide (4.1%) is about the same as the national average (4.6%).

In general, African Americans may be less likely to engage in suicidal behavior due to spiritual beliefs and religion. Religion provides an opportunity for social support (particularly for black women), and the strong belief that suicide is a sin may be protective. Unfortunately, related cultural beliefs about mental illness may prevent some African Americans from getting help. Research indicates that many African Americans do not seek treatment for depression even when they experience severe symptoms. Another contributing factor may be disparities in health care. Studies have found that African Americans are more likely than Caucasian Americans to get misdiagnosed and to receive poor quality health care.

NATIVE AMERICANS AND ALASKAN NATIVES

Suicide is the second leading cause of death for 10- to 34-year-old Native Americans, and the highest rates are generally among 15- to 24-year-old males. In a national survey, 16.9% of Native American high school students reported a suicide attempt in the prior year, which is significantly higher than the national average of 8.4% of students. For most other research reports, Native Americans and Alaskan Natives are combined into the category of "Other" racial groups, and thus we have less information on suicidal behavior for either of these groups.

Many American Indian tribes struggle with high rates of poverty, alcohol and drug use, and depression. Some research has identified the conflict between maintaining tribal customs and adapting to mainstream U.S. culture as a source of depression and suicidal thoughts. Additionally, many Native American tribes are located in rural areas with minimal access to health care, especially treatment that respects their culture. A few successful programs have, however, been developed to work with Native American youth. Such programs generally work within the culture of the tribe to increase peer support, connection to family, and spirituality.

LATINOS / HISPANIC AMERICANS

Suicide is the third leading cause of death for 15- to 24-year-old Hispanic Americans, but the highest rates are among elderly males (more than 85 years old). In a national survey, the number of Hispanic American high school students who seriously considered suicide was similar to the national average (17.9% vs. 16.9%), but more Hispanic American students attempted suicide (11.3% vs. 8.4%). Compared to Hispanic American men, women were almost twice as likely to report a suicide attempt in the high school survey (14.9% vs. 7.8%).

Studies show that many Latinos who have mental health problems do not seek treatment from a health care provider (less than one in five) or a mental health professional (less than one in eleven). Among people of Latin American descent, those born in the United States are most likely to experience mental health concerns. Research suggests that some U.S.-born Latinos may have conflicts between the language and culture of their family and the predominately English-speaking U.S. culture. Studies with Latinos who were born in other countries have found that religious beliefs, social support, and clear life goals can help reduce the risk for suicidal behavior.

ASIAN AMERICANS AND PACIFIC ISLANDERS

Suicide is the second leading cause of death for 15- to 24-year-old Asian Americans, but elderly men (over 85 years old) have the highest rates. A study that combined four years of survey data reported that the percentage of Asian American high school students who said they had seriously considered suicide (24.7%) or had attempted suicide (8.9%) was similar to the national averages (23.7% considered suicide and 7.7% attempted). Regrettably, Asian Americans and Pacific Islanders are often combined into the category of "Other" racial identity, and thus we have less information on suicidal behavior for these groups as well.

Some research has indicated that Asian American spiritual beliefs (such as Buddhist, Confucianist, and Taoist) may help to prevent suicidal behavior. On the other hand, some traditional beliefs about mental illness and suicide may discourage Asian Americans from talking about mental health and seeking help. Additionally, some Asian Americans have reported that language and other cultural differences present a barrier to effective health care.

Sexual Orientation and Suicidal Behavior

A number of research studies have shown that young people who identify themselves as gay or lesbian are more likely than their heterosexual peers to think about and attempt suicide. Teens who are attracted to people of the same sex have a higher risk for suicide attempts even if they have not actually had sexual contact with anyone. However, young people who have had sexual contact may have the highest risk of all. Studies have reported that between 18.5% and 42% of homosexual youth have attempted suicide.

You may be wondering what the reason is for this wide range of results. For starters, not everyone agrees about what qualifies as a suicide attempt, so different surveys use different terminology and therefore report different results. We also rely on participants in studies to report on their own sexual orientation. Again, the questions vary widely ("Do you identify as homosexual?," "What is your sexual orientation?," "Have you ever been attracted to someone of the same sex?"), which makes it difficult to determine if different studies are talking about the same groups. Finally, not all adolescents are certain enough about their sexual orientation to answer such questions unequivocally.

Why are lesbian and gay (and possibly bisexual and transgender) adolescents at such risk for suicidal behavior? We don't have a very good answer to that question. Some research indicates that homosexual youth who are depressed, anxious, use drugs, or have a history of sexual abuse have the highest risk. Other studies have shown that specific pressures faced by those who are gay or lesbian may increase their risk of suicide: Such pressures include, for example, telling other people about one's sexual orientation too soon, experiencing conflicts with family or others about it, sorting out one's own internal conflict about it, or deciding not to tell anyone about it at all. The current consensus is that *any* youth who face experiences that marginalize, reject, isolate, or victimize them are more likely to develop the negative emotions and coping patterns that could lead to suicidal behavior.

Mourning the Thousands

For all the limitations of our data about one group or another—black, white, Asian, Latino, native, and so on—we know one irrefutable fact: Far too many of our young people are at risk for suicide, and far too many have died by their own hand. I mourn for the 4,000 or more young people that we lose to suicide each year, and for the thousands who stayed alive but felt so terrible that they thought about suicide or attempted to kill themselves. Each and every suicide attempt and suicide that I hear about is like an arrow through my chest. I cry as I read their stories in the news, understanding all too well the desperate emotional chaos that they have suffered. What *causes* these behaviors? I believe that the desire to die is fundamentally a desire to stop intolerable pain, but the sources of this pain are complex. Science can help shed light on the origins and causes of suicide, but only personal experience can speak to the day-to-day terror and torment of wanting to die. To try and capture the complete picture of a suicidal crisis, in the next chapter I'll continue with my story so that we can see how the science of suicide might play out in real life.

> I believe that the desire to die is fundamentally a desire to stop intolerable pain, but the sources of this pain are complex.

Chapter Two
The Background Story

Every crisis has a background story. Whether in therapy or on the written page, I often find it hard to revisit everything that led up to my suicidal crisis. The negative parts of my past come to mind relatively easily, but they are difficult to think about for long, and to be honest, I procrastinated writing this chapter for that very reason. Many experiences in my past remain painful to me still; I cannot tell them in a linear way as a result. Then Dr. Brent asked about my early positive experiences, and I realized that I had neglected to consider them when initially planning this book. This oversight was interesting, perhaps the result of focusing so much on a subject, suicide, that by its very nature is bleak. Stepping back a bit, though, I can recall much that was positive in my past, and I believe it is important that I not forget that here. Nor should I forget to mention the extent to which certain traits in my being—strengths of personality, if you will—helped me to navigate the world I knew as a child and the world I've come to know as an adult. In short, while you need to know what set the stage for my crisis, I also want to introduce you to aspects of my life that, in time, set the stage for my recovery. Perhaps as you read my story, you will take the time not just to focus on your own painful memories, but also to remember your own strengths and positive experiences. Your recovery depends in part on embracing those as well.

What are "strengths of personality"? Or more basic, what is "personality"? Whole books have been written on this topic, but, in brief, the concept of personality describes an individual's unique pattern of emotions, thoughts, and behaviors. Personality is a mix of inherited tendencies and individual experience in the world. How much of our personality is attributable to our genetic makeup (our nature) and how much to the particular environment—the social world of our families, friends, communities, and so on—that surrounds and nurtures us is hard to determine. Many researchers have spent their entire careers on just such a question, but for our purposes in this book, all we need to know is that our inherent personality traits, along with brain chemistry and other biological factors, interact with our environment to make us who we are. In this chapter, I'll try to characterize the pieces of this "interaction puzzle" generally, using my own experiences as illustration, and to shed light on the extent to which the various pieces of the puzzle may or may not put someone at risk for suicidal behavior.

Intelligent and Spirited Child Meets Urban Black World

This could have been the headline for my personality development. Let's focus initially on the first half of the headline: the child, the young person named DeQuincy Alexander Lezine. Who is he? What are his traits?

I have always been a quick learner, with intelligence and creativity that reminded my parents of past family members.

Some of my paternal uncles painted beautiful still-life scenes, while my father preferred drawing with pencils or charcoal. In childhood, my brother and I learned how to draw and mix colors by imitating our father's work. On my mother's side, there weren't many artists, but they performed well in academics. Intelligence and creativity are generally positive, and I was rewarded with good report cards and special academic opportunities (such as entry into "gifted and talented" classes) for displaying those qualities. On the other hand, the value of certain personality traits depends on the scenarios in which they reveal themselves. Outside of school, I employed my intelligence and creativity to find mischief and figure out how to get away with it. In particular, I took to petty theft, enjoying the toys I snatched as well as the rush of avoiding capture. Of course, sometimes my parents caught me, having somehow noticed toys lying around the house that they didn't buy.

Like some other artists, I also had a tendency to experience very intense emotions. Some writers have referred to this tendency as an "artistic temperament." (As an aside, one research study showed that a group of creative writing students had much higher rates of depression and alcoholism in their families than did a comparison group of history students, and there is evidence that many artists and musicians in history may have dealt with depression or bipolar disorder. There may, in other words, be some truth to the idea that internal emotional turmoil and creativity are somehow linked.) When I was happy it felt like euphoria, but when I was sad it felt like a black hell. When I was angry, my rage was like a wildfire absolutely consuming me until I was just too burnt out to keep going. Maybe those were

When I was happy it felt like euphoria, but when I was sad it felt like a black hell.

early signs of bipolar disorder, the diagnosis I would be given years later, but back then, no one thought that children could be vulnerable to this illness. Instead, as a youngster, I was said to have inherited the fiery Lezine spirit that had characterized my family for generations. That spirit sometimes landed me in the principal's office for fighting, and my dad warned me about the violent rage that ran in our family.

I did find, however, that this particular inheritance could sometimes be positive. When channeled toward a particular goal, my anger could do more than just get me into trouble—it could serve as a motivator. Thus, I was at my best in the face of a challenge. For as long as I can remember, I believed that I could learn how to do just about anything if I had the chance. As I tried to control my temper, though, I tended to keep to myself and a few close friends. I was, and still am, an introvert. I liked— and in fact, needed—to have some time alone and some space to sort out *I was, and still am, an introvert.* my thoughts. Although like most of the kids in my neighborhood, I enjoyed a good game of basketball, I probably spent more time reading and drawing—solitary activities. I was also, like many kids, teased and bullied by peers. Those experiences reinforced my preference for staying away from social groups and approaching social situations cautiously.

When circumstances did not involve a lot of other people, I continued to seek out new and interesting experiences. As I said earlier, I thought of myself as an explorer. Aside from that, I always needed to find new things to see, or do, or learn. Otherwise, I got bored. My dad tells this story about me interrupting him one day while he was fixing a friend's car for some extra money. He looked up and there was Alexander, walking up the driveway well before school was supposed to be out. When he asked me why, I said I was bored, so I left. This kind of action based on frustration provides an example of my more impulsive nature. That incident, paired with high IQ test scores, landed me in the gifted classes so I'd stay engaged in school.

Personality Traits and Suicide

RISK FACTORS

I've now told you about some of my basic personality traits: intelligent, creative, highly emotional, aggressive, introverted, easily bored, and so on. Some of these traits are positive, but some bought me a lot of trouble, especially later when they became part of the dynamite that exploded my freshman year in college and sent me into a suicidal tailspin. They were, in fact, among the "risk factors" for suicide that I mentioned previously. As a reminder, a risk factor is a circumstance or event that increases the likelihood that a person will suffer from a given illness or disorder or will be predisposed to some kind of harm. (For instance, smoking is a risk factor for lung cancer.) Although we probably don't know enough about the relationship between personality and suicidal behavior, especially for young people, certain traits do seem to increase the risk of suicide. Certain combinations of risky traits can be especially dangerous. For instance, I liked seeking out thrills and "adventures," but I also spent a lot of time by myself, so there were few people around to help me stay out of trouble. This combination became all the riskier during my adolescence.

Certain combinations of risky traits can be especially dangerous.

Let's look at the most identifiable personality traits that may increase the risk of suicide:

- *Impulsivity* is the tendency to take action based on a certain feeling or situation, without giving it a lot of thought. Sometimes—for example, when making an "impulse buy" of candy or a magazine while in line at the grocery store—the consequences are minor. At other times, the consequences can be severe—for example, impulsively attempting suicide after breaking up with a boyfriend or girlfriend. Research studies consistently report that people who are prone to take impulsive actions in general are more likely to attempt or die by suicide, especially when they are adolescents or young adults. Scientists have linked some forms of impulsivity to the imbalance of certain chemicals in the brain, and the trait may be inherited.
- *Novelty seeking* is a predisposition to seeking out new information, pursuing rewarding experiences, and exploring new or exciting activities. Someone with this trait is likely to be curious and creative, but also have a low tolerance for frustration, a quick temper, and impulsivity. Like those with the more general trait of impulsivity, novelty-seeking individuals are more likely to take quick action based on frustration or anger, leading to higher risk for suicide.
- *Reactive aggression,* a tendency to experience emotional and sometimes aggressive reactions to situations, is closely related to impulsivity. Aggression in response to perceived threats or provocation is very different from calculated aggression designed to achieve some specific goal (which is known as *proactive or instrumental*

aggression). Reactive, defensive, or emotional aggression has a stronger association with suicidal behavior. When faced with a threat or frustration, people with reactive aggression may strike out, or they may injure themselves. This type of aggression has also been connected to brain chemistry and may be an inherited trait.

- *Introversion* is a tendency to be socially reserved, quiet, and primarily concerned with one's own thoughts. Over decades of research, introversion has been identified as a partially genetic trait with a strong association with suicide. Imagine a spectrum of behavior, with introversion on one side, and extroversion (being highly social) on the opposite side. Someone who is closer to the introversion end of the spectrum is described as an *introvert*. Introverts like me enjoy spending time alone or in the company of a very small group of trusted friends.

- *Harm avoidance* is a predisposition toward avoiding punishment, and it is closely related to introversion. When someone is very concerned with avoiding harm, he or she is likely to develop anxiety or pessimism about the future, to be fearful of uncertainty, and to anticipate and fret over problems that may or may not come to pass. This type of pessimistic worry has been linked to depression and suicidal behavior. Sometimes the person may be trying to escape from a perceived threat, and other times the person might attempt to escape from persistent and painful anxiety.

- *Social inhibition* refers to a tendency to withdraw from social situations or to experience discomfort around groups of people. As you might expect, people who are high in introversion or harm avoidance generally have this trait as well. Unfortunately, it can lead these people to a state of self-defeating, emotional isolation: Without social support, they might ruminate over suicidal thoughts, finding themselves unable to escape from their increasingly dangerous frame of mind. Additionally, for those with a small circle of friends, each loss or conflict with a friend may have a greater impact than it would otherwise.

- *Neuroticism,* or emotionality, means the tendency to experience negative emotions like anxiety, anger, and depression, especially under stress. Someone who is highly emotional may be more likely to perceive situations as threatening or stressful. In psychology, this degree of emotional instability is referred to as *level of neuroticism.* As you might guess, this trait is closely connected to harm avoidance, in the sense that it is also manifested in the effort to stay away from the negative feelings. This trait is also connected to both mood disorders (such as depression and bipolar disorder—more on those later) and to suicide.

Protective Factors

Of course, there are also traits that might protect a person from suicidal thinking or behavior. A person who has tendencies that are opposite to the traits I've just mentioned will at least avoid those particular risks for suicide. Some research studies have examined traits that not only lower risk, but also may actually protect a person from suicide. At least three traits deserve mention as potential protectors:

There are also traits that might protect a person from suicidal thinking or behavior.

- *Extroversion* is a tendency to enjoy and seek out social interactions. Extroverts are generally friendly, outgoing, assertive, and talkative. As a result, they are likely to have large social networks. With many friends and contacts, extroverts may have more opportunities for getting social support if they become depressed or suicidal.

- *Optimism* is a positive view of life. The optimist believes that people are generally good and that events will turn out well in the future. Such a perspective is likely to stop hopelessness and depression from setting in when something does not go well. Unlike the pessimist, who sees negative outcomes as inevitable and permanent, the optimist is more likely to meet disappointments or frustrations as they come along and to see them as temporary.

- *Transcendence* is the sense that one is connected to something larger than oneself—usually a feeling of a religious or spiritual nature. Some scientists believe that this characteristic can be protective, but we need more research on this possibility.

Turbulent Beginnings

Let's now look at the other half of that headline a few pages back: the world of my childhood, urban Los Angeles. Like many Americans, I grew up in a working-class household. We moved around a lot. The earliest home I remember didn't have much of a lawn, and I played games with my older brother in a backyard of dirt and charred grass in a small area enclosed by chain link fences. During one period, we lived in a downstairs apartment on the back side of a lot, with an elderly, distant relative upstairs and cousins in the house at the front of the lot. After school, my brother and I would play with our cousins or go to their place to have chilled Kool-Aid in plastic cups while we watched Michael Jackson videos or kung-fu movies.

I remember only a few events clearly that punctuated my early childhood. Mostly what stand out are the emotional or dramatic ones, like my mom adopting the neighborhood cat, Midnight, or my dad chasing one of our cousins down the street with a pocket knife. The concept of family was confusing. I knew that my family loved me, but I also felt like I needed to be cautious around them.

For a while, our primary babysitter was our paternal grandmother. I loved the smells of fresh baked chocolate chip cookies that often wafted through the halls of her house. Even with the persistent scent of cigarette smoke, the promise of chocolate was always welcome. Most days I was content with cookies, playing hide and seek near the cactus gardens, or admiring the seemingly endless spider webs that populated walkway bushes. Yet my most vivid recollections continue to muddy the concept of family. I have memories of a cousin showing me plastic lawn bags filled with shredded hundred dollar bills from drug sales gone bad. I recall my grandmother threatening to shoot one of my uncles because he stole her money.

Aside from all the drama, a pervasive sense of hopelessness hung in the air. I will never forget my paternal grandmother saying that there were only two kinds of people in the neighborhood: "niggers and Mexicans." We were the former, and she said that nobody from our neighborhood would ever "amount to shit." She wasn't trying to put us down, though; that's just how she saw the world. A lot of people in my neighborhood accepted that they would just live and die in similar circumstances. Like my grandmother, they just believed that was reality. But it wasn't a reality I could accept.

Fortunately, there were others who thought I could do better, like my maternal grandmother. I always liked her, even though she spent more time drinking, smoking, and gambling in Vegas than she did visiting us in Los Angeles. I remember visiting her in Chicago, where she told me that whatever I wanted to do—play soccer better or get an A in class—she believed I could do it. My mom also believed in us (my brother and me), and wanted us to be happy. She was full of good humor and taught me to laugh at the hard times in life. But Mom had her mood swings, too, and she was a thrill seeker— an unfortunate combination that can often lead to substance abuse. Leaving the family when I was young, she got caught up in a web of alcoholism and drugs. When she left, everyone in the family took it pretty hard. I'm not sure if it was conscious or not, but at that point I started losing my faith that everything would turn out okay. (I'm happy to say that eventually my mother overcame her substance abuse, and she just celebrated 15 years of recovery from addiction.)

My dad tried to help me develop my abilities, and to balance telling me I was smart with trying to cultivate humility in his son. Dad struggled with academics early in his life, and he had to overcome stuttering and a poor education to teach himself how to read well. Once he did that, though, he read voraciously and became a book collector who encouraged his sons to never stop learning.

My relationship with my father was complicated. In many ways, he was my role model. He was a hard-working man who kept his children and worked even harder when our mom left. Dad taught me how to play basketball, sketch and cartoon, repair the house, and clean—basically all the essentials I would need as an adult. My dad, brother, and I would go out fishing and just sit by the side of the water, our butts growing numb on the rocks while we laughed at each other's jokes.

It wasn't all good times, though. Dad had a dark side, particularly after my parents got divorced. Although he eventually stopped drinking, back then he would have a few bottles of Olde English 800 (a 40-ounce malt liquor beer) and lecture us for hours about all the things that could happen to us on the streets. We had to watch out for gangsters, thieves, pickpockets, drug lords, slum lords, con artists, bullies, prejudice, government. I can't remember the specifics of most of the tirades. Most of the time I was thinking, *I'm cold and sleepy, and my legs are getting really tired of standing.* Sometimes, though, we were just scared. Having your father's size-12 boot on your head as he "demonstrates" how the police treat black people tends to generate some fear. Then there were the whippings—or beatings—we'd receive as punishment. He lashed me with powerful strokes of a leather belt or extension cord, leaving welts that lasted at least through the following day.

When he suspected that we were harboring angry thoughts of vengeance, Dad growled that if we ever tried to retaliate against him, he would kill us. *I brought you into this world, and I can take you out.* Maybe he'd sneak in at night, he told us, and slit our throats while we slept. Everybody has their personal demons. What experiences had scarred my father so badly that he thought he needed to do this to his children? I don't know. I just knew that I *had* to get far away from home as soon as possible.

I just knew that I had to get far away from home as soon as possible.

My social life was also a mixed bag. Our family practiced Christianity as Jehovah's Witnesses, attending services three times a week. There are few greater comforts in the world than the belief that there is a higher power that cares about your well-being. I also had a caring extended family through my congregation. When we visited Mexico, we were treated like family by the Jehovah's Witnesses there, in spite of racial and language differences. Yet outside of our organization, we were ostracized and put down for our beliefs. Childhood seems to magnify our differences. Aside from my religion, other differences marked me for ridicule: I was the smart kid without name-brand clothes, the tall kid who stuck out in class photos, and the kid who had to go straight home after school. Having a spiritual family counteracted some of that negativity and helped keep me away from alcohol, drugs, and other trouble. Having teachers and counselors who encouraged me to keep learning and pursue higher education helped keep my self-esteem up. Still, the constant teasing and ridicule hurt.

Like everyone else, I just wanted to find a group of peers where I would fit in. It seemed like whenever I did find a small group of friends, either they would move away or my family would move. As a result, few friendships seemed to last more than a few years. Between the ups and downs with family and the uncertainty of relationships with peers, my initial tendency toward being an introvert was reinforced on a regular basis.

Social Environment and Suicide

RISK FACTORS

Environment is defined as the external surroundings that affect one's development and behavior. As I mentioned, our social environment incorporates our families, our friends, our communities—in short, the people with whom we interact and form relationships. As a result, the social environment in which we live has a trcmendous impact on our lives. And as with personality, research has identified some social situations that increase one's risk for suicidal behavior. Unfortunately, I experienced quite a few of these situations. Some create long-term risk, and others may suddenly trigger a suicide attempt or make an attempt more deadly.

The social environment in which we live has a tremendous impact on our lives.

- Generally, *negative life events* (including abuse, legal or disciplinary trouble, divorce, death of a parent, loss of a friend, loss of a boyfriend or girlfriend) may trigger suicidal feelings. These types of stressors can overwhelm someone's coping ability, particularly when the stress is new or unfamiliar. But no matter how old we are, we can learn how to cope with traumatic or stressful experiences, sometimes with the help of others, like therapists or clergy.
- *Family conflict* or ongoing fights and arguments between a parent and child can create both long-term risk and immediate thoughts of suicide. Some children develop suicidal thoughts following major arguments, separation from a parent, or the divorce of parents. Other children may develop depression, anxiety disorders, or problems with alcohol and drugs—factors that increase the risk for later suicidal behavior. In general, children are more sensitive to parent conflict, while teens are more sensitive to peer conflict.
- *Child abuse and neglect* might be considered severe forms of conflict. Often, the person who mistreats the child is

a family member or another trusted adult. Abused adolescents face a terrible dilemma: Someone they love has violated their trust and wounded their mind or body. People who have endured abuse or neglect as children are at greater risk for developing emotional problems, psychiatric disorders, and suicidal behavior as adolescents or adults.

The Suicide Potential of Childhood Scars

Child abuse is a legal term that is defined by each state based on some federal guidelines. There are generally four types of child maltreatment according to state law:

- *Sexual abuse* or *exploitation* includes having a child perform sexual activities, assist an adult with sexual activities (e.g., fondling genitals), or pose for sexual pictures. Other examples include exposing kids to adult sex, child prostitution, and child pornography (including related Internet communication).
- *Physical abuse* includes aggressive actions that injure a child, such as hitting, kicking, burning, pushing, or biting. In many states, physical punishment (using painful force to discipline a child without the intent of injuring the child) is not considered child abuse. However, lashing out in anger (severe physical punishment) can quickly cross the line and become abuse.
- *Neglect* is defined as a pattern of failing to provide for a child's basic physical, educational, and emotional needs. These needs include adequate food, clothing, medical care, and schooling.
- *Emotional abuse* or *verbal abuse* includes actions intended to intimidate (yelling, threatening, bullying), belittle, blame, ignore, reject, or exploit a child. As of this writing, emotional abuse is included as child abuse in every U.S. state and territory except Georgia and Washington.

(continued)

Child abuse and suicidal behavior

In general, child abuse is associated with adolescent and adult suicidal behavior (both attempted suicide and death by suicide). Research indicates that adults who were abused as children may be up to 25 times more likely to attempt suicide when compared to adults who were not abused. One study reported that 30% to 40% of teens who had died by suicide had a history of abuse, whereas only 2.5% of teens without suicidal behavior had a history of abuse.

Not all types of abuse convey the same degree of risk. Across research studies, child sexual abuse consistently carries the highest risk for suicide attempts. Most studies report that physical abuse also increases the risk for attempted suicide, though the relationship is not as strong as it is for sexual abuse. We know very little about the potential effects of neglect and emotional abuse because very few studies have looked at their association with suicide.

Traumatic experiences and suicide risk

While abuse itself might trigger suicidal behavior, more often it is the trauma—the long-lasting emotional wounds—that conveys future risk of suicide. As we learn more about the biological mechanisms that link trauma with suicidal behavior, it seems that repeated exposure to trauma may be the key factor that overwhelms the brain's stress response and radically alters our personalities. The result could be damaged self-esteem, depression, and chronic anxiety. Someone trying to cope with the memories of abuse and the painful consequences of trauma might start drinking more alcohol, take street drugs, or ultimately attempt suicide.

- *Bullying* (peer conflict) seems to be associated with suicidal behavior in both the victim and the bully, but probably for different reasons. The kid who gets bullied might not be accepted by peers and feel lonely or depressed. The bully, on the other hand, might push other kids around because he or she has low self-esteem or is not engaged in school. However, the research on bullying and suicidal behavior is relatively new and is not yet conclusive.

- *Suicide clusters* are groups of suicide deaths that appear to be linked in some way. Generally, a cluster of suicides may take place among youth who are not closely connected to one another, but who have experienced the same exposure to a suicide. If teens find out about a family member's or a friend's suicidal act and are not given adequate and sensitive support as they deal with their grief, then the loss might start a new suicidal crisis in young people who were already at risk for suicide (because of depression or other factors). This effect is amplified when media reports glamorize, sensationalize, oversimplify, or present grisly details of suicidal behavior. Reporters and communities now have access to information, through Web sites like the Suicide Prevention Resource Center (http://www.sprc.org), about how to handle the aftermath of a suicide.

- Suicide death is more likely when *lethal means* (such as guns or potentially toxic medications) are readily available. Many impulsive suicide attempts, facilitated by quick and easy access to a gun, result in death that might not have been truly intended. Just to be clear: If a parent owns a gun (especially a handgun), stores it without a proper lock, and keeps it loaded or has ammunition nearby, then that parent is providing quick and easy access. Everyone in the house, including a suicidal adolescent, could use that gun. If I had had quick and easy access to a gun during my suicidal crisis, I'd be six feet deep instead of writing this book. In addition, given easy accessibility to illegal drugs or prescription medications, many young people have died of an overdose. The bottom line is that families can help prevent suicide just by taking sensible precautions with dangerous weapons, drugs, and chemicals. Schools can take similar precautions—for example, by posting security around campus and barring access to tall places from which a person might jump.

PROTECTIVE FACTORS

Obviously, some risk for suicide could be reduced by changing the negative circumstances just described. However, there are also some social situations that seem to protect people from suicide.

- *Social support* could protect someone who is depressed or suicidal from taking self-destructive action. At the least, someone who feels connected to a social group (family and friends) might avoid attempting suicide because he or she doesn't want other people to suffer as a result. But social support is probably more effective when someone feels that others genuinely care and is engaged with them in positive and healthy activities. As I said earlier, it is dangerous for a suicidal person to be alone with his or her thoughts, but simply being in a room full of other people will not lift that person out of despair. What can help is active, engaged social support in which others in the room attempt to connect mean-ingfully with the person in trouble, try to alleviate the person's sense of hopelessness, or think through pos-sible options or ways that the person can cope better.
- *Family support* is critical for the healthy development of a child, and over the longer term, it may help protect that child from feeling suicidal later on. Of course, the

concept of family support is trickier for adolescents who, as part of their natural development, are struggling between wanting support and desiring independence from their families. So, while a family can help "protect" a teen or young adult from feeling suicidal, I believe it is important to strike a balance between being available to offer consolation and supporting a young person's quest for autonomy.

- There are two other social situations that might protect young people from suicidal behavior. Those who are *engaged and interested in school* are less likely to attempt suicide. Similarly, teens and young adults who are involved in a *supportive religious community* may be protected from suicidal crises. Some people decide not to attempt suicide because they believe that suicide is a sin, or they have other moral objections to suicidal behavior. When paired with support in getting help for underlying problems, this can be protective. (On the other hand, a fear of being shunned by the community can be a stressor.)

The Hidden Background Story: Biology and Genetics

No discussion about suicide and suicide prevention would be complete without acknowledging the role of biology. The biology of the brain is too complex for me to cover in detail here, but there are some key concepts that help to shed light on suicidal behavior. In this section, I will briefly introduce those con-

No discussion about suicide and suicide prevention would be complete without acknowledging the role of

cepts and conclude by telling you why the underlying biology is so important.

Neurotransmitters and Hormones

Much of the human brain is made up of specialized cells called *neurons* that keep in close contact with each other. One way that neurons communicate is through *neurotransmitters.* Generally, each neurotransmitter fits into a receptor like a key in a lock. And each neurotransmitter sent by the brain is like a note passed in class. Although the message on the note is the same, the response you get will be different if your friend receives the note or if the teacher intercepts it. Similarly, many neurotransmitters work with different receptors, and each type of receptor could generate a different response.

There are at least three neurotransmitter systems that play a key role in suicidal thinking and behavior: serotonin, norepinephrine, and dopamine. Imbalances in these systems, especially serotonin, are also implicated in many psychiatric disorders or problem behaviors, including depression, anxiety, alcoholism, aggression, and even problems with sleeping. A large group of serotonin neurons located in the lower center of the brain transmits information to parts of the brain responsible for thinking, planning, memory, and various other functions. So, low levels of serotonin in certain areas of the brain could push someone to consider suicide by impairing the person's ability to think and generate alternative ways to solve problems. Lower levels of serotonin are also related to feelings of distress and to increased risk for impulsive or aggressive actions, including suicidal behavior. Both genetics and our environment help to determine the level of serotonin that we have in our brains.

In addition to neurotransmitters, the body has chemicals called hormones. Hormones are primarily used for long-distance communication within the body. If neurotransmitters are like notes, hormones are more like cell-phone calls. With cell phones, a call goes out into the airwaves, is relayed by special towers, and is then received by the intended person. Similarly, many hormones travel from one organ (such as the brain, pituitary gland, adrenal glands, and so on) to others via the bloodstream, relaying information to specific receiving cells.

The main hormone system that plays a key role in suicidal behavior is called the *HPA axis*. The HPA axis is named for the three organs involved in the communication chain: the hypothalamus (H) and the pituitary (P) gland in the brain, and the adrenal (A) glands near the kidneys. The transmission of hormones between the hypothalamus, pituitary, and adrenal glands is primarily used to respond to stress—particularly events that are perceived as threatening, such as a car crash or a physical assault. This stress response is also connected to the brain regions responsible for memory, so that the brain can learn from stressful experiences and modify its response as necessary. Additionally, perceived threat (whether real or not) causes a chemical called *cortisol* to be released. Small bursts of cortisol help the body react to threats, but too much cortisol can negatively affect the memory and planning functions of the brain.

The other hormones that deserve some mention are the sex hormones: estrogens (associated with female qualities) and androgens like testosterone (associated with male qualities). While the primary role of sex hormones is to determine and regulate gender development, they also influence some brain receptors. These brain receptors could be related to suicide because they are involved in various mood and thinking functions. For example, testosterone has been linked to aggression (which is more characteristic of males), whereas estrogen increases in puberty have been linked to depression in adolescent girls. If you recall, there are gender differences in suicidal behavior. Part of the difference might be related to sex hormones, but that is just one theory (out of many) that still needs to be tested. To complicate the picture, both hormone systems (the HPA axis and the sex hormones) interact with the serotonin system, and serotonin interacts with the other neurotransmitters as well. As I said, humans are complicated, and scientists are only beginning to unlock some of the secrets of the human brain and body. For now, we still don't know how all of these systems interact with one another.

Genes and Environment

How do we end up with our unique biological makeup? Some of it is inherited through genes, the building plans for the body. And some behavioral tendencies seem genetically influenced as well. Several types of research studies indicate, for example, that some susceptibility to suicide runs in families. However, children could inherit suicidal behavior through genetics *or* through observing and learning the behavior from family members. In order to tease out the relationship between inherited risk for suicide and environmental risk, scientists have studied identical twins (who have 100% of the same genes) and fraternal twins (who have 50% of the same genes). Scientists identify a person who has attempted or died by suicide and then find out whether the person's twin (whether identical or fraternal) is more likely to also have exhibited suicidal behavior. Study after study reports that both identical twins are more likely than both fraternal twins to have engaged in suicidal behavior—suggesting that there is a strong genetic basis for suicide. On the other hand, identical twins could share almost identical environments growing up, which might mean genetics *isn't* so important. But then, in another type of study, one directly comparing genes and environment, researchers have shown that the children of parents with suicidal behavior are more likely to also have suicidal behavior even if they are raised by an adopted family with no suicidal history. The basic conclusion is that there is definitely a genetic component to suicide. What seems most likely is that genes contribute to long-term risk of suicide through their role in developing psychiatric symptoms or impulsive aggression.

The environment does certainly affect our behavior, but interestingly, it also interacts with our genetic makeup to influence our biology. First, while genes set the "starting point" for our development as humans, environment modifies what happens to us afterward. Second, environment can modify how or when genes affect our biology. Sometimes a gene lies dormant, not affecting our development at all. But an environmental factor such as an infection or an extremely stressful episode can "activate" or "switch on" that particular gene. This effect can be seen as early as during pregnancy, when the health of the mother affects the developing infant. A mother can promote her baby's brain development by eating healthy food and making sure that she gets enough of the proper vitamins. A stimulating and nurturing environment can promote healthy development, while abuse, trauma, neglect, and other stressors can harm the fetus. Alcohol or drug use by the mother, for example, can have a long-lasting negative impact on the infant's brain and body. Other negative experiences can alter the level of

An environmental factor such as an infection or an extremely stressful episode can "activate" or "switch on" that particular gene.

serotonin and cortisol in the unborn child's brain and affect the functioning of the HPA axis.

Why does all of this talk about biology matter? I'll give you four reasons:

1. We know that some risk for suicide starts very early because genes and other factors before birth are related to later suicidal behavior. Suicide prevention can start early.
2. We know that if environment and experience can change our biology in ways that increase suicide risk, then alternative experiences and nurturing environments can counter that risk.
3. We know that if biological or chemical imbalances in the brain are related to suicidal thinking and behavior, then other chemicals (like medications) might be able to restore our balance and help us avoid suicide.
4. We know that we are not destined to die by suicide no matter what our genes say. Genes don't explain everything, because environmental factors will affect the actions of our genes. Thus, even identical twins don't lead identical lives. Nobody is destined to die by suicide.

"Escape" From L.A.

When all is said and done, genes, environment, and personality (which is one end product of the combination of genes and environment) contribute to our risk for (or protection against) suicide through the thinking patterns that we develop. Because humans are so complex, we all end up with unique blends of positive and negative thoughts that shift and change over time, and it can be remarkably tricky to study these kinds of thought patterns.

I had a lot of beliefs about myself and the world that formed the basis for my future suicidal crisis, and they're a good example of how thought patterns can lead us into a downward slide toward suicide. When things were going wrong, as when my mother left the family or when I failed an exam, the soliloquy from my subconscious might go something like this:

Of course, no matter what you achieve, it won't be enough—for them or for you. Maybe you're just not working hard enough. Maybe nobody loves you, and nobody will ever love you. How could they? You're unlovable. Don't ask me why—there are a million reasons why people will never really like the real you. Your family didn't even want you around—a problem child. At school, you're a nerd, a reject, an outcast. That's why nobody wants to listen to what you have to say, so just keep it to yourself. Nothing you could say or do would ever help you fit in.

Is that a tear? Suck it up. Don't you know that real men don't cry? Hell, no. You can get angry, but all those other feelings are useless. Forget about them. You can't let them see you cry. If you cry, then people will know that they hurt you, that you're soft. If they know, then they WILL hurt you more. You can't trust anyone to not hurt you. You can't rely on anybody but yourself. Now pick yourself up and pretend you're not the worthless little shit that you are.

You can probably see how this type of thinking could easily lead to suicidal feelings. By the time I was a teenager, I had become a really great self-critic. Fortunately, I didn't always feel that I was worthless. There were times when other beliefs were active, such as when I got an award or got accepted to college, and then the internal dialog would swing to the other extreme:

> You did it again. You're a fighter. If you just have a chance, you can do practically anything. I know you can. Of course, there are a lot of people who doubt what you can do. Who cares? Forget them. You'll prove them all wrong. You will always have your spiritual family, and God will not abandon you even as things seem just about hopeless. He did not abandon Job, and He did not abandon Jesus. Besides that, you will always have your art. Drawing is such a wonderful diversion. You can make it. Hold on, Quix. A fresh start and good times are right around the corner. Once you get to college, all of this will be behind you, and you'll have the rest of your life to enjoy. Just hold on.

Unfortunately, when I got to college, a number of my protective factors and beliefs, those of the confident fighter, gradually disappeared as I faced all kinds of new social and academic pressures. Some protection I lost because my assumptions about my problems as a kid were wrong. For instance, I had thought that I didn't have many friends because my family kept moving around and because I couldn't do after-school activities. In my first weeks of college, I tried to be much more social, but it was exhausting. I realized that not having a huge group of friends might have more to do with me than with all that moving, and I had to come to terms with being an introvert. Three thousand miles away from home, having moved yet again, I did not have easy access to those I knew back at home. I didn't have my beloved older brother and my friends to help me get through tough times. I didn't have an easy way to get to the local Kingdom Hall where Jehovah's Witnesses met together, so my religious community was virtually inaccessible to me. My friends, family, and spiritual family faded into the background.

A surprising amount of suicide risk seemed to have followed me through the ivy-covered gates of the university. The emotional chaos that I had totally blamed on my environment back in L.A. turned out to be at least partially inside of me, and I hadn't expected that. I thought that I had escaped from the mental illness that plagued my family, but instead I had packed it with me for college. Eventually the delicate balance between risk and protection gave way, and the weight of the pressures I felt overwhelmed my crumbling defenses. I had held out against my suicidal potential for years, but I couldn't hold out any longer. I snapped.

Chapter Three

Inside the Suicidal Mind

N ow that we have talked about what a suicidal crisis looks like (Chapter 1) and about the background that set the stage for that crisis (Chapter 2), it is time to take a trip deep inside the suicidal mind. This is the only way to fully grasp the thinking, feeling, and behavior of the suicidal state.

Darkening Thoughts

As my situation deteriorated that freshman year in college, whatever self-confidence I had disappeared, and I became more and more pessimistic, jaded, cynical, and hopeless. College life was supposed to be different from my life back in Los Angeles. After all, I didn't travel 3,000 miles to experience the same alienated crap I had to deal with at home. I had come to escape the pain and find some happiness. I was trying to be more social, but that wasn't consistent with my introverted nature (though I had yet to accept that). I tried to make sense of the isolation. Why couldn't I have more friends? Why was college, my last hope, failing to bring me happiness?

I started thinking that maybe everything was just going to turn out wrong no matter what I tried. If I worked really hard to connect with people, I might be able to minimize the number of things that turned out wrong, but that was about the best I could hope for. I started to lose touch with most of my friends from Los Angeles. Sure, it was partially my fault for not initiating regular contact, but I focused on *their* failure to communicate. All of those yearbook entries saying, "Let's keep in touch," were obviously B.S. Apparently all good things, from those friendships to my feelings of joy or success at getting into a prestigious university, had to end. I began to think that I was just going to be lonely for the rest of my life.

I started thinking that maybe everything was just going to turn out wrong no matter what I tried.

My dad had had scattered and relatively short-lived friendships, too. Instead of socializing, he spent most of his free time on solitary activities, like visiting bookstores. *Like father, like son,* I figured. *No wonder Dad didn't trust people. My own mother left me, and then we kids had to fight against the drug addiction for her attention.* I loved my dad, but I never knew if he was going to be my loving and fun father or my angry and menacing father on any given day. I thought of it this way:

If you can't trust your parents, and your friends always seem to vanish, who the hell can you trust? There are some good people out there, but they leave eventually, it's just a matter of time. Why should I love anyone when it would only lead to heartbreak? Why should I tell people what's on my mind? Nobody really cares about me, although some pretend to. I can't afford to get too attached to anybody. As soon as I let my guard down, they'll hurt me—someway, somehow, someday.

My thoughts grew darker and darker. It was an unfortunate and vicious cycle, a vortex sucking me down into depression. The more I came to believe that my life was filled with pain, the easier it was to identify painful situations in my past and current life—and the harder it got to remember the positives. The bad situations reinforced my pessimistic beliefs. As you might imagine, it got to the point where I started to think there was little or nothing to look forward to. My problem-solving abilities shut down, and I saw no point in even trying to solve the never-ending problems of life. I was on a dangerous path. I'd wake up in the morning thinking, *I wonder what kind of pain awaits me today? Maybe I don't want to keep living in pain every day, waking up to new headaches. Maybe I could be done with life now. Maybe I should kill myself. There's no other way to stop this painful existence. Suicide is the only way out of this.*

Negative Thinking and Suicide

Everybody experiences problems and setbacks, but how you think about them dramatically affects how you feel about yourself. I've already touched on this a bit in previous chapters, but it's worth revisiting.

Everybody experiences problems and setbacks, but how you think about them dramatically affects how you feel about yourself.

Imagine, for example, two kids who are teased by the same bully in the same way. Kid #1 says to himself, "That bully's pretty messed up. He's really got issues. I can't wait to change to a different class where things will be better." Kid #2 says to himself, "If I wasn't such a geek, that bully might leave me alone. I should get used to this, because I'm going to get pushed around for the rest of my life." Obviously, it's not quite that simple, but which kid do you think goes home feeling bad? If you said, "The second kid, of course," then you're right.

Many research studies have demonstrated that certain ideas about what causes negative events are related to depression and suicidal thoughts. Those ideas fall into three types of explanatory thinking:

1. *Internal* causes: If you have a negative view of yourself, then you might blame yourself when bad things happen.
2. *Global* causes: If you think the world is generally a negative place, then you might think that most situations will turn out badly.
3. *Stable* causes: If you think the future is usually going to be bad, then you might believe that negative events will keep happening to you.

In the earlier example, the second kid thought that he was bullied because of his own characteristics (internal), and that the experience would be similar over time even in different places (stable, global). Everybody has these beliefs sometimes, whether or not they have any basis in reality. However, for some people, this pattern describes their *usual* way of thinking, their *general* approach to life. In Chapter 2, I talked about this type of thinking pattern as a pessimistic personality trait. Someone who is this pessimistic about the future can quickly become hopeless. Although my cynicism sort of protected me from blaming myself for my misery, I still believed that my world was a negative place that probably wouldn't change—so I became hopeless.

Someone who is hopeless might start to think about suicide as an option. In fact, research has consistently indicated that unresolved hopelessness is a good predictor of suicidal thinking and future suicide attempts. The dictionary defines *hope* as a belief that what you want can actually be obtained, or as an aspiration that you have something to look forward to. Imagine being without this! Life seems pretty dismal without hope. If you've had the good fortune to never feel hopeless, I'll help you to empathize with this experience:

> Picture in your mind whatever makes you most happy. Maybe it is an activity that you love to do. Maybe it is spending quality time with someone you love. Now, imagine all of that being taken away, forever. How would you feel? What would you be thinking?

This might be close to the type of hopelessness we're talking about.

Research also indicates that people who are suicidal may have difficulties with problem solving, particularly with various relationship problems. However, not all research studies have found this to be the case. One explanation is that, at least for some of us, we are quite capable of solving problems most of the time, but we find it more difficult (or don't even try) to do so when we are depressed or hopeless. Whatever the reason, some people who develop a negative outlook on life also have problems with maintaining relationships. You might recall from Chapter 2 that people who keep to themselves, or who are uncomfortable in social situations, have a higher risk for suicide. Well, once again, people who have difficulties working through interpersonal problems might be at greater risk for suicidal behavior.

For years, therapists and other clinicians have said that suicidal people seem to have a narrow focus (constriction) that ends up centering on suicide as a solution, to the exclusion of all other options. They based their observation on careful examinations of suicide notes and on years of working in hospitals or clinics. I know I experienced such constriction as I became increasingly hopeless. However, we don't have much research on this aspect of problem solving. As you might imagine, it would be difficult to find people who are considering suicide, at the precise time that they are making this life-or-death decision, and get them to participate in a research study.

The most dangerous thing about considering suicide, especially in a constricted state of mind, is that it can lead us to act on what we hopelessly perceive or believe to be real in the short term. If someone believes that the only way out of debt is to die, then he or she might attempt suicide, even if tomorrow's winning lottery ticket was sitting in a coat pocket. Remember Shakespeare's *Romeo and Juliet?* Romeo impulsively kills himself because he believes his love to be dead, even though she was alive all along. He was fooled by his own perception, and then he made an irrevocable decision based on the flawed perception. It happens in real life, too.

Painful Emotions

I don't remember which came first for me during the fall of my freshman year in college, the negative thoughts or the onslaught of emotions. In many ways, it doesn't matter, since they fed into each other in fueling the suicidal urge. Some thoughts or memories are incredibly painful. Some emotions lead to thoughts of escape. Like a lot of guys, I believed that feelings just get in the way most of the time—so I tried to avoid them. Sooner or later, though, they came back with a vengeance.

... I believed that feelings just get in the way most of the time—so I tried to avoid them. Sooner or later, though, they came back with a vengeance.

The sadness hit first. I remembered all the hurt I had endured over the years. I wanted to cry for the little boy whose mom had left, and the boy who spent days working instead of playing with the neighborhood kids. I felt the pains of the daily peer torment I suffered during junior high school, and again in high school. It hurt all over again to get hit in the back of the neck with spitballs and to know the shame in comparing my hand-me-down shirts to the new Tommy Hilfigers others wore. Sometimes I was sad because I just felt so damn lonely. Even when I wasn't alone, I felt like I couldn't trust most people enough to really feel connected to them. Sure, I was an introvert, but even introverts like to feel like they have a few close friends. At college I longed for companionship, and looked with envy at the socialites and happy couples. But the fact was I could have had hundreds of friends, and it wouldn't have mattered if I didn't sense I could connect with any of them. As it was, the friends I had felt somehow farther and farther away from me with each passing day. That's one of the truly frightening aspects of depression—it's like losing your eyesight; the world's still out there, but you can't see it anymore. I was in a dark place, and I did not believe that even my close friends could fill the void. It all hurt so much that my heart plummeted. I hid in darkness or walked alone at night so that nobody could see my shameful tears. I was worried about being seen in that state; I believed people would tell me that I was less of a man because I was crying.

To the outside world, I pretended that nothing bothered me. I didn't tell anybody that I was so terrified of my father's violent rage that I continued having trouble sleeping at night even when I got to college, waking to each small noise. Those sleepless nights only made my state of mind worse. I started worrying about things that didn't really exist—FBI surveillance, imminent war, vicious animals leaping out of the night shadows. I was paranoid. It doesn't matter whether or not those things were real; we react to what we perceive to be real. My mind was going a mile a minute trying to figure out how to prepare myself for those hazards. We couldn't have guns on campus, so I bought knives—about thirty of them. The vigilance was absolutely exhausting sometimes, but I couldn't afford to let my guard down.

So many bad memories, but because I couldn't describe them openly without crying, I got angry. The volcanic fury tore through my veins, consuming me. The anger flashed up so quickly—I could feel my eyes narrow, brow tightening, lips curling, heart racing, temperature shooting through the roof, fists clenched for action. A few times I lashed out, and my friends had to stop me from getting into fights. Most of the time, I plotted quietly, with a brooding, murderous bitterness lurking beneath the surface. The bitterness sat atop a baseline of anger at the world for constantly trying to mess with me, and anger at my parents for abandoning me.

Emotional Dysregulation and Suicide

Research indicates that painfully negative emotions (sadness or depression, anxiety, anger, guilt, loneliness, shame) contribute to suicidal thinking. Of course, we've all experienced negative emotions, so what would make them so bad that someone would consider suicide? Here is empathy exercise #2:

> What feeling or emotion is the hardest for you to tolerate? I mean the emotion you avoid or try to change as quickly as possible. Sadness? Anger? Fear? Now, imagine feeling that way all day long, just about every day, week after week. Imagine

becoming convinced that this absolutely intolerable feeling would never go away no matter what you tried. The feeling plagues you, crowding out your other thoughts. All you can think is, "I need this to stop now!"

That's fairly close to the type of psychological pain we're talking about.

In Chapter 2, I introduced the concept of "emotionality" or "neuroticism" as a personality trait. More broadly, any intense emotional reaction to events can increase the risk for a suicide attempt. Someone who is highly emotional may have problems with relationships or difficulties with coping under stress. Some researchers refer to this state as *emotional dysregulation,* meaning difficulties (dys) with controlling (regulation) the emotional response to events. Studies have linked emotional dysregulation to history of child abuse and other traumatic experiences. In terms of biology, the overactive emotional response may be connected to changes in how the body's stress response (the HPA axis, discussed in Chapter 2) and the brain's emotional memory centers are activated to deal with threats—perceived or real. With this connection to biology and personality, it is possible that some people are more prone to developing emotional dysregulation than others. Fortunately, if traumatic experiences can create difficulties with handling emotions, then therapeutic experiences can help people learn how to restabilize their emotional responses. I'll talk more about that, and about prevention and recovery, in Chapters 4 and 5.

> Someone who is highly emotional may have problems with relationships or difficulties with coping under stress.

The Look of Private Hell

I thought there was no way out of my despair. I was at a great university, trapped in a private hell, dying from the inside out.

In desperation, I tried to drop hints to those around me about the extreme pain that I was in.

In desperation, I tried to drop hints to those around me about the extreme pain that I was in. I played music with lyrics that screamed about depression, loneliness, anger, hopelessness, escape, and suicide. In my music class, I wrote a piece entitled "Young Suicide." I changed my clothes, replacing khaki with black, and exchanging royal blue for blood red. I often wore a hood, and I almost always tried to shade my eyes with a baseball cap even while in class. I put more themes of angst and sadness into the comic strip I did for the student newspaper. I sat in the back of class or in obscure corners of the cafeteria so that I wouldn't be noticed. More and more I withdrew from life, avoiding social situations when possible. I just wanted to escape. Of course, it wasn't all black and white. I gave off mixed signals, still smiling and laughing most of the time, still visiting with friends or acquaintances. Initially, I took a certain pride in trying to hide my heartache. I didn't offer up my suicidal thoughts for discussion, and nobody asked. As time wore on, friends noticed more and I more explicitly revealed my desperation.

Adolescents and young adults sometimes reach out for help in unusual ways, and sometimes they reject help when it is offered. While I was writing this book, a young college student in Virginia shot and killed 32 of his classmates, and wounded many more, before killing himself. Before his suicide, he sent a videotape to the news media, which aired after the massacre. Much of what was on the tape was incoherent, but one thing he said caught my attention. He said that there had been plenty of opportunities to prevent the incident—opportunities that were missed most likely by classmates, professors, and college officials. Reports indicated that many people on campus were afraid of him. Would things have turned out differently if someone had seen this young man as scared instead of scary, or troubled instead of troubling? The fact is that many people did take notice of him and tried to intervene. At one point two years before the incident, he was ordered to seek mental health treatment on an outpatient basis, but there was no indication that he sought or accepted it. If someone had been able to convince him to pursue treatment—what would have happened?

At the peak of my suicidal crisis, once I had resolved to die, I felt I was beyond help. And then, suddenly, I felt nothing. Or rather, I had an odd sensation of peace. Motivational speaker and author Catherine Traff aptly captures this sensation in the title of her book, *The Calm Before the Storm.* Imagine a hurricane, which may be immediately preceded by clear, lovely weather—then all hell breaks loose. For us, the storm represents the suicidal act, and the calm that precedes it is the peace that we feel once we've finally decided to die. Sometimes people use the materials at hand and attempt suicide as soon as the notion occurs to them. Sometimes suicide requires more planning. In my case, as described in Chapter 1, I had to gather the right materials and figure out a way to say goodbye to people. I went about doing so carefully, methodically, and above all, calmly.

We usually end up doing a lot of things right before we leave home for a while. Maybe you arrange for the mail to be held at the post office, or forwarded to a new location. Maybe you get someone to take care of your pets, plants, or home. You might tell important people that you are leaving. Once I had made the final decision to kill myself, I started telling people directly that I was going away—that I was actively getting ready for my expedited death.

Warning Signs, Redux

In Chapter 1, I briefly mentioned the warning signs that might indicate a person is considering suicide. Now that we have more context, we can talk about those signs of distress in more detail.

- *Mood changes.* Generally, distress is associated with the experience of negative emotions, particularly when those emotions become overwhelming (in other words, psychological pain). Someone might cry more often (sometimes seemingly without a reason) or just look more sad than usual. On the other hand, a sudden switch from negative moods to happy or peaceful feelings may also indicate danger, if there isn't a good explanation for the change. As I just mentioned, I felt incredibly serene and my mood lifted once I resolved to kill myself, because I was no longer struggling with ambivalence.
- *Anger and rage.* Sometimes pain and suffering hide behind angry masks. For some, the anger will be extremely apparent with outbursts, shouting, and possibly fighting. Others will maintain a quieter, brooding rage and simply appear more irritable than normal. Anger may have two effects: First, it is a negative emotion that can contribute to psychological pain; and second, it activates the HPA axis, gearing up the body for immediate action. There are few acceptable outlets

for rage, so many people may feel trapped with this emotion. Because anger also pushes for an immediate response, sometimes it can lead to violence against others or against oneself.

- *Anxiety or agitation.* Another emotional state that activates the HPA axis is anxiety. Someone who is anxious might appear to be more fearful, jumpy, agitated, or cautious than usual. When anxiety or fear is focused on something specific (for example, a masked man with a gun), then it can help with a short-term and appropriate response (run). However, like anger, anxiety is a negative emotion that might push for an immediate and self-destructive response to a situation (whether or not there is really a threat). Long-term anxiety can also be exhausting, and some people may start to long for death rather than suffer through another anxious day.

- *Lack of purpose or reasons for living.* While negative thoughts and emotions create higher risk for suicide, reasons for living (like goals and joys in life) can protect against suicidal action. Someone who has specific goals in life has reason for hope, and probably has motivation to find a way through problems that come up. If these reasons for living disappear, hopeless desperation might emerge. Research has confirmed what we might already know intuitively, that people who are suicidal can come up with fewer or weaker reasons for living.

- *Feeling trapped.* As someone becomes increasingly suicidal, the options for coping with stressful situations and painful emotions seem to evaporate into thin air. The important thing to remember is that it doesn't matter if there really *are* a lot of available options. If a person doesn't *believe* there are other options, then he or she is likely to feel trapped. Eventually, when we feel like there is no way out, we get desperate. Suicide might eventually seem like the only way out.

- *Withdrawal from friends and family.* Many people who are thinking about suicide withdraw from the people they care about. A suicidal person may feel like a burden on others and seek to remove that burden. In my case, I got tired of reaching out to people, and wanted to see if they would care enough to reach out to me. When I was closer to attempting suicide, I thought that my death would be much easier (for me to accomplish and others to accept) by adding some emotional distance.

- *Hopelessness.* People who become hopeless might give up on activities that they used to enjoy, talk about giving up on a goal or dream, or otherwise paint a gloomy picture of their future. All the other warning signs are generally not lethal as long as someone still has hope. We can withstand terrible emotional pain if we believe it will eventually stop. Some people withdraw from family and friends for a while to work on some solo project, knowing that they will be reunited later. Most of us could even stand feeling trapped as long we knew that we would eventually find a way out. Once hope leaves, however, everything changes. People who believe that their pain will never end, or that it is impossible to find a way out, are much more likely to consider suicide. In hopeless desperation, many have preferred to seek death rather than face

> *All the other warning signs are generally not lethal as long as someone still has hope.*

a life of pain. Many research studies have found that people with a wide variety of psychiatric disorders or distress are much more likely to be suicidal if they are hopeless.

- *Substance abuse.* Some young people experiment with alcohol and drugs for temporary pleasure, and some use these substances for another reason: escape. For many, though, substance use ends up not being enough of an escape for several reasons: (1) the effects run out; (2) people build up tolerance (in other words, they need more of the substance in order to obtain the same effect); (3) stress and problems aren't really solved, so they continue to plague the person when he or she is sober; and (4) substances have their own costs in terms of money, risk of getting arrested, and so on. The young person who turns to drugs and alcohol to get away from painful situations and emotions is also someone who might turn to suicide as a final escape. In fact, research consistently shows that people who abuse alcohol and drugs are also more likely to attempt or die by suicide than those who do not.

Drugs, Alcohol, and Suicide

Drugs (including alcohol) work by altering the neurochemistry of your brain and body. Many of the drugs that people use act on the brain systems that are responsible for feelings of relaxation, reward, and positive emotions. Usually, we get these naturally pleasurable sensations from tasty foods, exercise, or sexual orgasms. Both drugs and natural pleasures tend to involve the neurotransmitter systems of dopamine, serotonin, glutamate, gamma-amino-butyric acid (GABA), and natural opioids (chemicals found in the brain). Dopamine and

(continued)

serotonin are also associated with suicide. You may recall that the neurotransmitter systems interact with each other, so, for example, drugs that primarily affect the neurotransmitter GABA may also cause changes in the dopamine or serotonin system. At the biological level, this may help to explain why drug use is associated with suicidal behavior.

Most drugs either induce relaxation (such as depressants like alcohol) or excitability (such as stimulants like cocaine). Some people who are already depressed or suicidal may use relaxation drugs to calm themselves. On the opposite side, someone who is using stimulants may be more likely to make an impulsive suicide attempt in reaction to a negative event.

In the bigger picture, some people who regularly use drugs or alcohol tend to run into problems that could, in turn, trigger suicidal thoughts. Aside from possible legal problems, chronic substance abuse could start to interfere with someone's ability to work or have meaningful relationships. To deal with this stress, some people start using even more drugs, creating a vicious downward cycle that is in itself stressful. Sometimes the drug-related stress could trigger thoughts of suicide.

- *Reckless behavior.* While some youth turn to drugs and alcohol to get away from their problems, others engage in reckless behavior. There's a good reason why people who consistently do risky things are said to have a death wish—some do. Sure, there are many young people who are thrill-seekers, but shouldn't we ask why they are willing to gamble with their lives? We should pay special attention when someone who usually doesn't take life-threatening risks starts engaging in reckless behavior. For example, when a cautious young man like me suddenly starts running across the interstate or sitting in the middle of street, there's a good chance that he is not looking for a good time. He may be suicidal.

- *Suicidal ideation.* Finally, outward evidence that someone is thinking about suicide is, of course, the most direct warning sign about suicide risk. If somebody talks, sings, writes, jokes, blogs, or in any other way communicates about suicide, then that may mean he or she is at least thinking about it.

Psychiatric Disorders Related to Suicide

You might be asking why I chose to talk about psychiatric disorders last in this chapter, since most books on suicide put this topic right up front. After all, research consistently shows that mental illness is associated with suicidal behavior. I've waited to approach this topic for two reasons. For starters, while most youth who die by suicide could be diagnosed with a major psychiatric disorder (60%–90%), most youth who have been diagnosed with psychiatric disorders *do not* die by suicide. So I don't want you to think that having a psychiatric disorder is the main reason one might attempt suicide. Also, by talking about other factors first, I can put the role of psychiatric disorders in context. Absence of diagnosis, or treatment for a diagnosis, does not equal absence of risk for suicide. Some people without a diagnosable psychiatric disorder attempt or die by suicide. Some of them may have had some psychiatric symptoms, but not "enough" to "qualify" as a disorder. Some might have become overwhelmed by life and, without hope for a better future, attempted suicide. By discussing the other factors first, I hoped to provide you with some common concepts that could apply to someone who is suicidal whether or not he or she has a diagnosed disorder.

That said, let me now briefly describe several individual disorders and their connection to suicide (there are also excellent books available about individual disorders; see the Resources section of this book).

Depression may be the first disorder that comes to mind when you think about suicide.

- *Depression* may be the first disorder that comes to mind when you think about suicide. We've all experienced some degree of sadness—for example, when someone we love dies, when someone or something disappoints us, when we're so stressed out that we don't even know where to start to get things done. Some people experience much more, though. Where everyday sadness or grief is like a swimming pool, theirs is like an ocean. However, there is more to this disorder, officially called major depression, than just sadness or despair. Imagine turning on your favorite television show or doing your favorite hobby and not getting any joy out of it. Depression creeps through a person's entire body, affecting the way he or she eats, sleeps, moves, thinks, and feels. The hallmark of depression is painful sadness or despair, but it also disrupts a person's self-confidence, self-esteem, and ability to make decisions. Research has consistently found that depression is associated with both suicide attempts and suicide deaths, particularly for women.
- *Bipolar disorder* (also known as manic depression) involves periods of major depression alternating with periods of either mania (e.g., an intense euphoric high) or mixed states—a combination of the two. Whereas things tend to slow down in depression, everything

speeds up in mania. When manic, people tend to think and talk much faster than is normal. They might become hyperactive, often seeking out pleasure without paying attention to the possible consequences (risky behaviors include promiscuous, unprotected sex, spending too much money, reckless driving, and more). Because their minds are racing so fast, people may have difficulty with concentration and decision making. While you have probably heard about the more euphoric form of mania, other forms that many people with bipolar disorder experience are intense irritability and agitation. And in a mixed state, a person could have, for example, manic energy paired with depressed thoughts. Whether or not the mania and depression occur at the same time, almost everyone with bipolar disorder will experience both the ups and the downs. Bipolar disorder is not as common as depression, but research indicates that young people who have symptoms of bipolar disorder have a high risk for both suicide attempts and suicide deaths. Those with a mood disorder (depression or bipolar disorder) are 11 to 27 times more likely than others to die by suicide.

- *Schizophrenia* is a disorder that seems to disconnect a person from reality. Contrary to its popular use, the term has nothing to do with a split personality (which is an entirely different disorder). People who have schizophrenia have trouble controlling their thoughts, emotions, and behavior. They may have delusions— beliefs that are not consistent with reality. They might be convinced that people can hear or influence their thoughts, or that a particular group is intent on tracking them down to hurt them—this is known as paranoia. Sometimes people with schizophrenia might experience hallucinations, perceiving sounds or sights that are not really there. They may even hear nonexistent voices talking about them, or commanding them to do things that they don't want to do. Some people with schizophrenia may become so overwhelmed by the terror of paranoia, the frustration of not being able to enjoy anything, or the loneliness of living in a separate reality that they try to kill themselves to stop the pain. They might attempt suicide because they hear voices commanding them to do so, or they might take an action that unintentionally results in self-injury or suicide. For example, someone might believe he or she can fly, and jump off a building. Like bipolar disorder, schizophrenia is relatively rare, but when people start to experience such disorienting symptoms, research shows that they have a high risk for suicide.

- *Panic disorder* is a combination of panic attacks (periods of extreme anxiety accompanied by an elevated heart rate, perspiration, and even hyperventilation) and of a person's reactions to those panic attacks. If you were having a panic attack, you would experience a sudden and intense feeling of absolute terror. Your heart would start pounding furiously, you would break out in a sweat, your hands would tremble uncontrollably, and you might find it hard to breathe. Your chest might start to hurt as if you were having a heart attack, you might feel like you were choking on something, or you might feel so light-headed that you worry about passing out. Many people who experience these attacks worry about when the next one will strike, and they might start avoiding the places or situations that they believe cause the panic attacks. Some people with such overwhelming anxiety start to think of death as a way out. Research has shown that, particularly for young women, panic disorder and anxiety are associated with suicidal behavior.

- *Conduct disorder* describes a pattern of aggressive, destructive, or disruptive behaviors. Everyone goes through a rebellious period when young, but this disorder describes a long-lasting pattern. Someone with conduct disorder might bully others, use weapons, torture animals, start fires, vandalize property, steal, lie, and otherwise violate laws or rules. Some young people with conduct disorder see the actions of others as threatening (even when no threat exists), so they may react aggressively. Some research studies have found that youth, especially young men, with conduct disorder are at risk for suicide attempts and suicide. Up to a third of young male suicide victims have had a conduct disorder, but usually along with another major disorder.

Sometimes a person can have multiple psychiatric problems (known as *comorbidity*). For example, some people with conduct disorder or schizophrenia may also suffer from depression. Perhaps the most common overlap is that of a psychiatric disorder and substance abuse (a combination that is often specifically called a *dual diagnosis*). Unfortunately, though people with mental illness may abuse substances in order to ease their symptoms, street drugs and alcohol tend to make symptoms worse over time, partially because they make it even harder for the body to properly regulate chemicals in the brain.

Regardless of the particular set of psychiatric symptoms that someone experiences...

Regardless of the particular set of psychiatric symptoms that someone experiences, whether those symptoms are associated with a single diagnosis or with a set of comorbid conditions, it is crucial that they be identified and treated promptly and effectively to reduce their impact on the individual. Moreover, research indicates that the mental and emotional difficulties of psychiatric disorders make suicidal behavior much more likely, and this risk may only increase if the disorders are untreated. Generally, psychiatric disorders could contribute to suicidal thinking in a number of ways. Some people may experience painful emotions, such as sadness or anxiety, as symptoms of their disorder,

...it is crucial that they be identified and treated promptly and effectively to reduce their impact on the individual.

while others might feel sad or anxious about having a mental illness. Stress can also play a role, as psychiatric disorders make it harder to cope with stress. Sometimes people with a mental illness end up acting in ways that make life more stressful. Finally, decision making is often affected by mental illness. Many disorders make it harder to think logically, either by interfering directly with thinking or by increasing the tendency to react to powerful emotions.

Riding Out the Wave of Odds

I wouldn't have written this book if I thought it was impossible to resurface from the suicidal depths. I'll admit that a lot seems to conspire against doing so: What's in our past, our present, our surroundings, our minds, and our bodies can sometimes all rise up to so overwhelm us that just letting them drown us can seem like a viable option. However, we all have the ability to change, altering the course of our lives. Summoning that ability starts in the mind, with the decision to live. With that, we can begin to face our wave of overwhelming odds, adapt to it, and ride it out.

We cannot, however, ride it out alone. And we especially can't do it alone if all we're seeing in our mind's eye is our own funeral. Whether or not you realize it, you already know one of the most important steps for suicide prevention: accepting that you may be suicidal (or recognizing when someone else may be). Another step is telling someone about it—getting help. I didn't really get help until I was already deep in my suicidal crisis, and I nearly let my own wave of despair drown me. But when I finally did get—and more to the point, accept—help, I began, little by little, to resurface from my suicidal depths and, in time, to recover myself and my life.

Chapter Four

Getting Help

A s I look back on my life in Los Angeles, I recall that, even before I went to college, people around me knew that something might be wrong. I was sent to counseling on and off throughout junior high and high school, and I hated it. I thought therapists were just paid strangers who wanted to pry into my private life. I simply refused to believe I needed their help, and I refused to talk. The various school psychologists and therapists that I was sent to over the years barely register in my memory as a result. Unfortuna-

Unfortunately, in ther-
apy, if you say nothing,
you get nothing.

tely, in therapy, if you say nothing, you get nothing. Maybe if I'd given therapy a chance when I was younger, then I could have avoided my suicidal crisis. Perhaps if I had had some way to build up my coping resources in my early teen years, then I wouldn't have found myself in a life-threatening situation during college. I don't know, but if I had it to do over again, knowing what I do now, I'd try.

As that miserable first semester in college wore on, a small but growing group of friends became aware of how much distress I was in. They tried to support me as best they could—going with me to sports events, accompanying me at meals, writing me letters and e-mails with jokes, biblical scriptures—anything to try to cheer me up. Sometimes it worked, and I'd feel better for a little while, but it was usually short-lived. Nights were the worst. Even my friends on the West Coast (a three-hour time difference) had to go to sleep sometime. Alone, my thoughts eventually turned to the idea of suicide.

In the days leading up to my suicidal crisis freshman year, my friends were getting desperate and increasingly concerned that my feelings weren't a passing phase. Amanda, my best friend at college, told me that she was overwhelmed and didn't know what else she could do for me. She said that she would stand by me as I tried to get past the pain, but she needed help. Amanda had visited the university counseling center to ask for advice, and she encouraged me to go see a counselor. She offered to go with me, but I thought that would be too embarrassing, so I said I would go alone. I trusted her judgment, so if she said they might be able to help, then it was worth a shot.

On our campus, the counseling center was located in a ghastly white building that I approached with a sense of dread. I wasn't sure what to expect, and I didn't want anybody to see me going into (or leaving) the counseling center. At the bottom of the stairs, I hesitated, but thinking of my friend's encouragement to get help, I pushed on. On the second floor, there was a long walk down a narrow hall toward a deceptively plain door. It didn't look like much, and yet behind that door was where people poured out their pain for others to examine.

The receptionist asked if my matter was an emergency. What was I supposed to say? "Yes, I'm here because I want to kill myself, but I want a second opinion first." I'm sure I gave her some relatively ambiguous answer that was still clear enough for her to have a therapist see me right away.

This would be the first time I took counseling seriously. Dr. O. asked a lot of questions, but more importantly, she listened. She took a few notes during the session, but otherwise it would have seemed like a normal conversation—aside from the subject matter. She didn't sit behind a desk, and I didn't lie down on a couch. We both sat in chairs, and Dr. O. made me feel comfortable talking about how poorly things were going. She gave me the sense that she actually cared about what happened to me. She was remarkably friendly, and surprisingly, she didn't want to lock me up (which is what I really feared) as soon as I admitted being suicidal. We talked about it for a while, and then I promised to live at least until a second session the following week and to call her if anything changed. I fully intended to keep my promise, and I guess she trusted that. I left with a card that had written on it the date and time of our next appointment, as well as my therapist's name. I exited the counseling center quickly, but overall, therapy wasn't so bad after all. Amanda was relieved to hear that I had started the process.

This would be the first time I took counseling seriously.

Psychotherapy

Sometimes we need to work with a professional to resolve major issues with our mental health and personal lives. Mental health professionals are a group of people who spent extra time in school, and in practice, to become specialists in the type of mental and emotional issues we have been talking about in this book. Considering suicide is serious. It is easy (especially for others) to list reasons for living, but I know that you also have some powerful reasons for wanting to die. Choosing to take your own life is *the* critical decision; all other questions, decisions, options, choices—everything depends on how this turns out. But before making a major decision about suicide, probably the biggest decision of your life, you *deserve* to get advice from a specialist—a mental health professional.

Misconceptions about Psychotherapy

My resistance to therapy as a kid was at least in part due to my misconceptions about it. I didn't really know what to expect from psychotherapy (often called simply *therapy* or *talk therapy*) because I had heard a lot of different things about it. Generally, we get information about mental health and therapy from TV, friends, family, neighbors, church, the Internet, and so on. It is difficult to know what to believe. So let's start by clearing up some common misconceptions about therapy before discussing what it is really like.

1. *Therapy is just for "crazy" people; therapy is for people with "real" problems.* First off, most people use the term *crazy* as a quick way to dismiss mental health issues and not bother to examine the real problems that people face. Most would prefer to avoid talking or thinking about such problems, so they never learn how to address or resolve them. That you've picked up a book like this one suggests, though, that you're not one of those people, and I commend you for your bravery in examining the especially hard topic of suicide. What problems are supposedly "real" enough to

warrant therapy? I'd say that any mental or emotional problems that people are struggling to understand in themselves are real. And I'd say that if a problem is important enough for someone to think about dying, then it truly is "real" enough for therapy. Now, is therapy just for people who have a diagnosed mental disorder? No. Thousands of people without a psychiatric diagnosis go for therapy every day. Some people go to therapy not because they have a particular problem but because they want to keep improving their mental health and to learn more about themselves. It is just like other health issues. For example, people will exercise for different reasons: competitive sports, staying fit, losing weight, and so on. Well, different people go into therapy for different reasons, and they're all legitimate concerns.

2. *I'm (he's/she's) too sick for therapy to help.* It's never too late to get some benefit out of therapy. Even if you feel your situation is too far gone—if you've already made the decision to do something drastic, for instance, or if you feel you're beyond hope—that doesn't have to be the case. Therapists are specially trained to help people find a way out of bad situations, from the mildly troubling ones to the ones that could be disastrous. There are many types of therapy and many therapists available in most communities. There are very few people who would not benefit at all from *some* type of therapy. Besides, the good thing about therapy is that if one type doesn't work, you can stop and look for other options. It's worth a try.

It's never too late to get some benefit out of therapy.

3. *Real men don't do therapy; strong people don't go to therapy.* This one's especially for you guys out there: Chances are you've bought into a macho notion that our society just loves to perpetuate: that guys don't (or shouldn't) talk about personal problems. Men are even less likely than women to go to a medical appointment (which may be why women live longer). The basic idea is that men aren't as emotional as women are. Apparently, whoever invented this idea never saw the fans of the losing team after a championship game! Now that we have blogs and MySpace pages, the personal thoughts or troubles of men are more apparent than ever. Men might use different language ("I'm stressed out," or "I really need a drink"), but the needs are still there. If you play sports, then maybe you've had to do physical therapy after an injury. Well, when you experience an emotional injury so painful that you think about suicide, it is time for some psychotherapy. In case you're still concerned about your rep, you might feel more comfortable knowing that licensed therapists promise to do everything possible to protect your confidentiality and anonymity (in other words, they're not going to tell other people what you've been talking about, or even that you've been talking to them at all).

4. *Therapists are in it for the money; they don't really care.* I've heard this quite a few times as a therapist, and I said it myself when I was younger. Now that I've been on the other side of that statement, I can say without a doubt that most therapists are certainly *not* in it for the money. Aside from a few well-known people, counselors don't earn lots of money. Most of us could have chosen other careers that paid more. We chose to work

in mental health because we care. Just because your therapist seems composed and calm during the session doesn't mean he or she is less human. I've seen therapists cry after sessions, kick furniture in frustration, and work long—unpaid—hours trying to figure out how to help someone they are working with. Of course, I'm sure there are exceptions—therapists who, say, aren't as committed as they should be to helping their clients—and if you're finding that to be the case with your therapist, then find a new therapist. Your therapist should care, and it's important to be confident of that during your discussions about suicide. Your therapist will be scared—it is a scary topic—and he or she might make some mistakes in trying to get you help. Therapists are, after all, only human. The most important thing is that they care enough to try whatever they can to help you. Put another way, try to think less about whether or not your therapist is "in it for the money" and more about whether you are getting something worthwhile for your money—the chance at a happier and more fulfilling life.

5. *Therapists know all the answers; they can "fix" me.* Therapists are trained professionals, specialists in mental health, but they don't know everything. For one thing, they need you to tell them about the unique aspects of your case. They need you to tell them what you want, your goals (or your trouble identifying goals). They need you to open up so that they can help you. Therapy isn't something that is done *for* you; it's a process in which

Therapy isn't something that is done *for* you; it's a process in which you must be an active participant.

you must be an active participant. Unfortunately, for all of us, there are no quick fix answers. On the other hand, that means that each person's therapy is a little different, based upon each person's needs and goals for therapy.

Can Talking about Problems Really Help?

A while back, I talked about many different biological factors that can increase someone's risk for suicide. So you may be wondering—if suicidal thoughts are due to biological causes, how can simply *talking* about the situation possibly help? Well, therapy is not just "talking." It is an opportunity to learn different and hopefully healthier ways to perceive, respond to, and manage negative emotions, and to improve interpersonal relationships with others. These are some of the nonbiological aspects of suicidal ideation, and therapy can go a long way in helping you overcome them.

As we've discussed, your temperament and personality could increase your risk for suicide if you tend to have strong emotional reactions, or take action quickly without thinking things through, or are inclined to spend a lot of time alone. Therapy could suggest ways for you to get better control of your emotions, or to resist the temptation to take immediate action, or to identify support networks with people you trust.

You might be overwhelmed by stress right now. In that case, therapy might help you by suggesting ways to decrease stress, solve problems, or cope with unpleasant situations that you can't change. Your past traumatic experiences could increase the risk for suicide. Therapy can help you work through the emotional aftermath of trauma in various ways. Regardless of the cause, therapy might help you learn how to stop being so self-critical, self-loathing, self-defeating, or self-threatening (in other words, how to stop feeling suicidal). Basically, therapists work with us to figure out how to deal with problems (that come from the outside or inside) so that we can have a better life.

Different Types of Psychotherapy

There are many different options for therapy, and thus there seem to be endless ways to categorize therapy types. I'll start with who is in the room. At the very least, there will be you and your therapist. This is called *individual therapy*. If you add a significant other (boyfriend, girlfriend, etc.), and the therapist focuses on the relationship, then that is *couples therapy*. Sometimes an entire family (parents and kids) will work with a therapist in *family therapy*. Finally, a therapist might meet with an entire group of people—various individuals, couples, or families—in (you can probably guess by now) what's called *group therapy*.

Another way to think about the types of therapy is to identify the types of professionals you might see. When you think of therapy, you might immediately think of psychologists. Psychologists have had advanced training in dealing with mental health issues, and they have developed most of the types of therapy that are offered. However, other mental health professionals can provide therapy as well. The list of people you might go to for help includes psychiatrists, clinical social workers, mental health counselors, marriage and family therapists, and psychiatric nurses. Make sure that whoever you see for therapy has a license to practice therapy in your state. Strict licensing requirements have been established to make sure that providers meet a certain standard of care before offering you services.

A Who's Who of Mental Health Practitioners

Several different types of professionals provide mental health care; each group has its own educational and licensing requirements, and each practitioner has a unique set of skills he or she can use to help you get through a suicidal crisis.

- *Clinical psychologists* (Ph.D.) provide assessment and psychotherapy, or talk therapy, for mental and emotional disorders. Some psychologists specialize in working with adolescents or families.
- *Clinical social workers* (M.S.W.) provide talk therapy as well, but also tend to focus on improving conditions in one's environment that might be contributing to that person's problems.
- *Psychiatrists* (M.D.) are medical doctors who are trained to diagnose and treat mental disorders and emotional problems. Psychiatrists may specialize in one or more areas of mental health, such as child and adolescent psychiatry, and can prescribe medication if necessary.
- *Psychiatric nurses* (R.N. or R.P.N.) have received special training and certification in order to work with those suffering from mental disorders; in some locations, they can also prescribe medications.

There are also different schools of therapy in which therapists train to become specialized in a certain type of therapeutic approach.

PSYCHOANALYSIS AND PSYCHODYNAMIC THERAPY

The oldest school is called *psychoanalysis*, with a more modern form called *psychodynamic therapy*. Because this type of therapy has been around for a long time (it was originated by Sigmund Freud, someone you may have heard of), it is what you're most likely to see on television or in the movies. If you were in psychoanalysis, then your therapist would try to help you probe your innermost thoughts and feelings (your psyche) and interpret (analyze) how your past has influenced them. In psychodynamic therapy, your therapist would help you work out the interactions between past issues and current problems (dynamics). I tried psychodynamic therapy. It was helpful, but let me tell you, it is *hard work*. There is a reason why we push some things out of our minds. I had to talk in detail about the past I wanted to forget, and re-experience the emotions I wanted to stay numb. My therapist didn't let me hide behind humor or purely intellectual explanations when talking about painful experiences. This type of therapy could be useful in the long run, but in the short term, it could increase your depression and anxiety because it spotlights your troubles. I did other types of therapy to deal with my immediate symptoms first, and then did psychodynamic therapy later to develop a deeper understanding of myself. Most therapists who do psychoanalytic or psychodynamic therapy don't do formal research, so there is less evidence about whether or not this method works for specific problems when compared to other forms of therapy. However, some studies have shown that brief psychodynamic therapy that focuses on relationship problems can help some people with depression.

COGNITIVE-BEHAVIORAL THERAPY

The second major school of therapy is called *cognitive-behavioral therapy* (CBT). If you were in CBT, then your therapist would help you understand how your thoughts (cognitions) and actions (behaviors) foster and maintain anxiety, depression, and other symptoms. In particular, your therapist would help you figure out what kinds of negative things you think about, or believe, out of habit (automatic negative thoughts). For example, I've mentioned believing that I was worthless, that nobody cared, and that I would never be good enough. When I was in CBT, my therapist worked with me to identify those types of beliefs and figure out ways to counter them. Many CBT therapists also assign homework—usually activities intended to help you break out of the habit of negative thinking more

If you were in CBT, your therapist would help you figure out what kinds of negative things you think about, or believe, out of habit...

quickly than through talk therapy alone. Obviously, your progress in CBT depends on how much you put into it—both in terms of your initial effort to identify your negative thoughts and behaviors and of your ongoing practice of the methods you learn to counter those habits. Many aspects of CBT are taken directly from experimental studies about human learning and emotions, so many therapists who practice CBT also have an interest in research. We have, as a result, a large amount of evidence showing that CBT helps people decrease negative symptoms (like anxiety and depression) and learn healthier ways of living.

INTERPERSONAL THERAPY

The third major school of therapy is called *interpersonal therapy* (IPT). If you were in IPT, then your therapist would help you identify the relationship (or interpersonal) issues that seem to trigger your symptoms (especially depression). You would then work with your therapist to learn the social or communication skills needed to resolve those interpersonal issues. For example, in IPT you might work on dealing with a continuing conflict with your parents, on coping with peer pressure, or on developing your own identity as you emerge as an adult. To benefit from IPT, you would have to practice, out in the "real world" where you're interacting with the other person or people, the skills you learned in therapy. Although IPT is newer than the other schools of therapy, there is research evidence that it can be effective for reducing depression.

OTHER TYPES OF THERAPY

There are many other types of therapy out there. For example, *problem-solving therapy* focuses on systematic ways to think through problems, while *solution-focused therapy* identifies behavior changes that could help you reach your goals. Most of the other types of therapy borrow from, or combine elements of, the three major schools. Some therapists will describe their style as *eclectic,* meaning they use techniques from a variety of schools. For instance, in my graduate program I received training in brief psychodynamic therapy and in CBT, eventually settling on solution-focused therapy as my main style. Being flexible and eclectic can be a good thing if the therapist is skilled in selecting the right techniques for the right problems. However, some therapists will say they are eclectic because they have a mixed approach that doesn't really fit any particular school of thought. Don't be afraid to ask the therapist for specifics about how he or she would approach your problem and how his or her recommended techniques are supposed to help.

When Suicide Is the Main Issue

Most therapies are not designed to focus specifically on suicidal thoughts or feelings—instead, they concentrate on factors that can contribute to those thoughts and feelings. In fact, for a long time, people who were suicidal could not participate in therapy research studies at all, but were instead referred for immediate help. However, two types of therapy focus directly on the topic of suicide. Research evidence has shown that they are effective in preventing future suicide attempts.

Dialectical-Behavioral Therapy

The first therapy for suicidal behavior is *dialectical-behavioral therapy* (DBT). In full DBT, you would have both group therapy and individual therapy. In your one-on-one sessions, your therapist would focus on the major issues that you faced during the week, working from controlling suicidal impulses to enhancing quality of life. In your group sessions, your therapist(s) would help you learn skills for coping with emotions and emotional situations. Earlier, I mentioned that some people become suicidal because of negative emotions that seem to come up too quickly, become too intense, or take too long to subside. With DBT, people learn skills to regain control of their emotional lives. DBT is similar to CBT in using homework and other activities (behaviors) to enhance learning. DBT is different from CBT, though, because it emphasizes a seemingly paradoxical balance (dialectic) between accepting yourself and trying to change. Most of the research showing that DBT helps prevent suicide attempts has been done with adults who had patterns of emotional difficulties. However, DBT has been successfully adapted for use with adolescents and adults with a variety of issues related to suicidal behavior.

Cognitive-Behavioral Therapy, Redux

The second therapy is a new version of cognitive-behavioral therapy specifically developed to help people who have attempted suicide. If you were in this type of CBT, your therapist would help you identify the stressful situations, negative thoughts or beliefs, and reactions that led up to your suicidal crisis. Then you would work with your therapist to figure out new coping strategies to avoid or tolerate stressful situations, challenge your beliefs, and adopt new solutions to feeling suicidal. CBT for suicide attempters is a brief therapy (about ten sessions) that is added on to other treatment. There is good evidence that this type of therapy helps prevent future suicide attempts, at least among adults. This form of CBT has only been around for a few years, so researchers are still conducting studies to find out if it can prevent suicide attempts in other groups as well.

Peer Support

Earlier I said that research had identified social isolation as a risk factor for suicidal behavior. On the opposite side, social support might help protect people from suicide. New research indicates that one's perception of social support and belonging makes more of a difference than the number of friends one has.

Self-help groups or *mutual-help groups* are structured forms of social support for people with a particular shared experience or identity. There are groups for men, women, LGBT (lesbian, gay, bisexual, or transgender) persons, teens who are pregnant, people who have experienced problems because of alcohol or drugs, and people who are coping with various psychiatric disorders. Groups have been established for individuals who have thought about suicide or attempted suicide, and for individuals who know someone (particularly a family member) who died from suicide, called survivor support groups.

The evidence suggests that mutual-help groups can assist people to feel less isolated and can increase their coping skills, enhance their self-esteem, and foster and maintain a hopeful outlook. If you're in college, then you can use your campus counseling center or student affairs office to find out what kinds of groups meet at your university. In junior high and high school, the school counselor or psychologist might know of local groups; the phone book and Internet are also good places to look for information on support groups in your community. You can also check out the Resources section of this book for information about nationwide groups that meet in local chapters.

Medication 101

So far, we've focused on the different psychotherapies available for dealing with emotional or social concerns that are connected to suicide. However, you'll recall that suicidal behavior has complex roots, including in one's biological makeup and brain chemistry. The purpose of prescription medication is to help regulate the chemicals in your brain and body that may have become unbalanced, leading to suicidal thoughts. Some people will feel much better with medication alone, but research has shown that for many other people, a combination of medication and therapy is more effective. If you are seeking professional help, you will want to work with your treatment provider to figure out the best treatment option—be it medication and psychotherapy or one or the other—for your unique case.

> The purpose of prescription medication is to help regulate the chemicals in your brain and body that may have become unbalanced, leading to suicidal thoughts.

Misconceptions about Medication

As with psychotherapy, you've probably heard all kinds of things about medications. As much as I didn't want to do therapy initially, I certainly didn't want to take prescription drugs. I had heard only horror stories about what those things did to people. As it turns out, they're not that bad, and you have much more control over them than you might believe. Let's clear up some common misconceptions about them before getting into the specifics about the types of medication available.

1. *Medication will make me a different person.* Let's be honest here, most drugs (prescribed or otherwise) don't radically change a person. Humans are just too complex. On the other hand, drugs will change certain aspects of how a person thinks, feels, or acts. Unlike street drugs, prescribed medications target biological areas that aren't working quite right. When things aren't going right, people feel like they can't enjoy life and that they can't do the types of things they would like to do. Most people feel *more,* not less, like themselves once they find medications that work.

2. *Taking medication is a sign of weakness; it's a crutch.* Taking medication is a sign that you recognize that something about your biology or brain chemistry could be working better and you're willing to do something about it. Medication is an option that you have for taking care of yourself. People with high blood pressure, diabetes, or other conditions take medication to help balance the chemicals in their bodies. Why should taking medication to help balance chemicals in

your brain be any different? Furthermore, for the record, I see nothing wrong with crutches. If I break an ankle, you can be damn sure that I'm going to get some crutches and not hobble around on my cast, risking further injury.

3. *Medications are addictive; the "industry" wants to get me hooked.* Most medication does not cause the type of biological dependency that professionals would describe as an addiction. (People do sometimes experience withdrawal effects if they stop taking some medications too abruptly, but these drugs are not addictive.) Honestly, aside from returning your ability to function well, most psychiatric drugs don't provide the kind of exhilaration or high that would be addictive. That said, there are a few addictive medications, and doctors do closely monitor those drugs. As for the pharmaceutical industry, well, these are profit-making companies, so I'd be lying if I said that they didn't have a stake in whether or not you take their medications. However, you and your doctor are free to select whatever option will be best for you.

How Can Medication Help Prevent Suicide?

In Chapter 2, I mentioned some of the biological factors that influence behaviors and feelings like reactive aggression, depression, anxiety, and suicidal urges. For example, serotonin plays a major role in both depression and suicidal behavior, so some medications help to restore the balance in a person's serotonin system, easing the suicidal urge. Other brain chemicals (neurotransmitters) that might contribute to the suicidal impulse include dopamine and norepinephrine, and there are medications available that target those systems as well. So you can see that some medications might have a direct effect on suicidal feelings.

Another way that medication can help is by reducing the types of mental and emotional problems that eventually push people to consider suicide.

Another way that medication can help is by reducing the types of mental and emotional problems that eventually push people to consider suicide. In Chapter 3, I mentioned some of the overwhelming emotions and psychiatric symptoms that could contribute to suicidal feelings. Someone might experience such terrible emotional pain that he or she wants to die, and medication could help alleviate some of that pain. In other cases, such as in people who have schizophrenia, the ability to think clearly may be impaired, and so medication could help improve their coping and decision-making capabilities.

Getting Effective Medication

To obtain a prescription for medication to improve your mental health, you would need to see one of the following types of providers: a psychiatrist, a primary care doctor, or a psychiatric nurse who's had advanced training. In a couple of states (New Mexico and Louisiana), psychologists who pursue additional training can get limited prescription privileges as well.

Like psychotherapy, medications are variously classified in different categories. At one time, they were mostly classified according to the disorder that they were designed to treat. Recently, however, medical providers have started to use medications to treat specific symptoms or problems regardless of the diagnosis (or absence of diagnosis). The movement to make health care more "patient-oriented" or "client-focused" has influenced this prescription approach. In other words, the belief has arisen that health care's ultimate aim should be to help you achieve your goals and to focus on overcoming the physical and/or mental barriers that stop you from having a meaningful life. I like that approach, so I'm going to present the different types of medications according to a similar organizational scheme. Because each medication has a generic name (e.g., fluoxetine) to denote its active chemical ingredient, and a brand name (e.g., Prozac) made up by the pharmaceutical company that produces it, I'm going to refer to both so that you can recognize both forms.

- *When you feel depressed,* your doctor might prescribe an antidepressant. Given the earlier discussion about neurotransmitters connected to depression, you might guess correctly that many of these medications target the serotonin system. Today, the selective serotonin reuptake inhibitor (SSRI) is a first-line treatment for depression. The medication acts only on serotonin (it is specific) by reducing (inhibiting) the amount of neurotransmitter that is absorbed by cells to be recycled (reuptake)—thereby increasing the level of serotonin in the brain. Common SSRI medications include fluoxetine (Prozac), sertraline (Zoloft), paroxetine (Paxil), and citalopram (Celexa). As your doctor will probably tell you, it can be a couple of weeks before you feel a major difference because the medication works through a complex chain of chemical events in your brain. I've tried a few different SSRIs. Though everyone will react differently to a given drug, I can say that for me, they were easy to tolerate, and they had a dramatic impact on how I felt. Some people may feel more agitated or hyper when they start taking SSRIs, but that generally subsides once their bodies adapt to the medication.

Do Antidepressants Cause Suicide?

Recently, the media has reported on research indicating that there may be an elevated risk of suicide in young people who take anti-depressants, especially the SSRIs. These findings have led to all sorts of debate on whether these medications are safe for young people to use, or whether SSRIs and other antidepressants actually cause suicide in some people. The short answer to that last question is probably no, but the story is more complicated than that. To more fully answer the question, let's focus just on the SSRIs and recall our earlier discussion about how they target serotonin. First, we know that serotonin is associated with suicidal behavior partially because of its role in our moods and in agitation or reactive aggression. We also know that SSRIs basically work by increasing the amount of serotonin available in the brain.

So let's work through what might happen when someone takes an SSRI. The medication increases the amount of serotonin available in the brain. Its main goal is to treat symptoms of depression, but the increased serotonin has other effects as well. Because brain receptors react to serotonin (and thus, also to SSRIs) at different times, a person can expect a variety of reactions to taking the medication. This is particularly true when someone initially starts taking the medication, because the body needs time to adjust to it. Most people will experience mild side effects, like headaches or diarrhea, but some people will experience increased agitation (due to increased serotonin). If someone does not feel less depressed *and* starts to experience rest-lessness and the urge to react strongly to negative events, then the risk for suicidal behavior could go up. That is the most accepted expla-nation for the effect, but it is still under investigation. Whatever the mechanism is, health or mental health professionals who prescribe medications (of any kind) need to monitor how each person responds, particularly in the early stages of treatment.

(*continued*)

Unfortunately, there have been times when health care providers did not follow up with a young patient regularly, and that adolescent became more suicidal. Such potentially tragic outcomes reinforce the need for careful prescribing practices and follow-up. In part, each health professional is responsible for monitoring how patients respond to treatment and for making adjustments to deal with side effects. However, you can help by going to follow-up appointments and telling your doctor (or other health care provider) about side effects as soon as possible. If you start feeling more agitated or suicidal after starting to take a new medication, notify your health care provider immediately.

Now let's look at the scientific research behind this now very public debate about antidepressants and suicide. In 2004, the U.S. Food and Drug Administration (FDA), the agency that regulates medications, gathered the available information about SSRIs and suicidal behavior from studies with young people. Altogether, there were 24 studies, involving 4,400 youth, and nobody died by suicide. However, 4% of young people taking an antidepressant reported suicidal thinking or behavior compared to 2% of youth who were taking a placebo. As part of his research, Dr. Brent and colleagues conducted an analysis of available data that showed only a very slight elevation in suicidal ideation among those taking an SSRI. In contrast, they found that 11 times more people benefited from the SSRI than became suicidal. Nevertheless, the FDA enhanced the warnings on the packaging of SSRIs (and other antidepressants) and encouraged health care professionals to monitor patients more closely. Some news outlets printed dramatic but misleading headlines, such as "Antidepressants double the risk of suicide" (remember, there were no suicides). Some pharmaceutical companies and health care providers issued defensive statements focusing solely on the benefits of SSRIs. The truth is just more complex.

The bottom line? Antidepressants are extremely effective in treating depression, one of the main factors that contribute to suicidal behavior. The risk of developing suicidal thinking or behavior because of an antidepressant is very low (4% or less). Again, if you work with your health care provider to monitor your response to antidepressants (or any other medication), you can decrease side effects (suicidal or otherwise) and improve the benefit you get out of the treatment.

You might recall that serotonin is not the only neurotransmitter that is associated with depression. Norepinephrine and the closely related brain chemical dopamine may also be involved, so some medications (called "newer antidepressants" because they were introduced in the late 1990s after the SSRIs) target combinations of neurotransmitter systems. The medication buproprion (Wellbutrin) acts on norepinephrine and dopamine, while medications like venlafaxine (Effexor) and mirtazapine (Remeron) target serotonin and norepinephrine. I've felt well on one of these medications for years now, after I stopped getting as much benefit from my SSRI (over time your body might start responding differently to the same medications). Some older types of antidepressants, such as monoamine oxidase inhibitors (MAOIs) and tricyclics, also work on multiple neurotransmitters, but with less specificity. As a result, the older antidepressants can be useful in some cases, but they also tend to have more side effects.

- *When you feel anxious,* your doctor might prescribe an anxiolytic (anxiety-relieving) medication. As I mentioned earlier, serotonin plays a role in anxiety as well as in depression, so your doctor could prescribe an SSRI or something like venlafaxine (Effexor) that targets serotonin and other systems. Some people with anxiety may benefit from a medication, like buspirone (BuSpar), that targets serotonin and GABA (one of the neurotransmitters involved in anxiety). Such medications are often highly effective at helping people control or alleviate various forms of anxiety. However, you might be more familiar with the medications known as benzodiazepines or "benzos," such as diazepam (Valium), alprazolam (Xanax), clonazepam (Klonopin), chlordiazepoxide (Librium), or lorazepam (Ativan). Those medications have been around for longer so they are most likely to appear on TV shows or in movies. (In fact, as I write this, I see that Valium is one of the only medication names that Microsoft Word automatically recognizes.) You might be surprised to find out that those medications are powerful sedatives that are tightly regulated under federal and state laws. Many people have become addicted to benzodiazepines, experiencing painful withdrawal symptoms when they run out of the drug. These medications are dangerous for another reason: It is possible to overdose on benzos.

• *When you can't sleep (insomnia)*, your doctor might prescribe a sedative or hypnotic. As you can guess from the name, hypnotics are named after hypnosis, the act of inducing sleep or a sleeplike state. The commonly prescribed hypnotics today include zolpidem (Ambien), trazodone (Desyrel), zaleplon (Sonata), and eszopiclone (Lunesta). Most of these newer hypnotics act quickly (within about 15 minutes) and only last for a few hours, helping you fall asleep without feeling extra drowsy in the morning. Some have found that diphenhydramine (Benadryl), the part of Tylenol PM that makes people sleepy, can help with insomnia. Like benzodiazepines, which used to be the primary medication for insomnia, many hypnotics target the neurotransmitter GABA. Although they are generally safer and less potent than benzodiazepines, some people get addicted to hypnotics as well; in fact, all sedatives have potentially addictive properties, and most are considered controlled substances under federal or state laws. They are best used temporarily and only when necessary. Your doctor or therapist can help you identify some nonmedicinal strategies for getting better sleep over the long term.

- *When you have trouble thinking, you're extremely agitated, or you find yourself disconnected from reality (in a state of psychosis),* your doctor might prescribe an antipsychotic medication. Much like the symptoms they are prescribed for, antipsychotics are probably the most misunderstood of the psychiatric medications. At one time, when we knew much less about psychosis, doctors primarily used antipsychotics like chlorpromazine (Thorazine), haloperidol (Haldol), thiothixene (Navane), or fluphenazine (Prolixin). These are known as the *first-generation antipsychotics,* and they work mainly by blocking the action of dopamine, one of the neurotransmitters. (By way of contrast, you may recall that some street drugs like cocaine work by increasing dopamine action, creating the type of disconnection from reality that people with untreated psychotic disorders can experience.) Regrettably, the old antipsychotics do more than just treat the psychosis; they create new problems, including heavy sedation, loss of muscle control, agitation, spasms of the tongue and jaw, and other side effects. It is partly these effects that fuel people's fears that psychiatric medications are mind-controlling or personality-altering substances.

Today, the most common antipsychotics are so different from the older varieties that they are called *second-generation antipsychotics.* Also called *atypical antipsychotics,* this group includes medications like olanzapine (Zyprexa), risperidone (Risperdal), quetiapine

(Seroquel), aripiprazole (Abilify), ziprasidone (Geodon), and clozapine (Clozaril). As you can tell from the long list of names, scientists have been quite busy trying to come up with improved treatments for psychosis. While the old antipsychotics could stop people from experiencing delusions and hallucinations, the new antipsychotics also help people with psychosis regain their ability to think clearly, experience a range of emotions, and generally enjoy life. They too have side effects, but generally they're not of the sort caused by the first-generation antipsychotics. The second-generation medications have improved the targeting of dopamine receptors and added effects on serotonin as well. Perhaps because of its effects on serotonin, clozapine (Clozaril) has been shown to help prevent suicidal behavior. The old antipsychotics aren't useless, though. With careful doses, many of them have proven extremely useful in helping people become less agitated, especially in the short term. During one summer, I was incredibly irritable and agitated. For some reason I just felt like I was angry with everyone and everything. It was an almost murderous rage that was hard to contain. My psychiatrist prescribed a small dose of an antipsychotic, which I took for about two months. It helped immensely.

- *When your emotions or moods change a lot,* your doctor might prescribe a mood stabilizer. The first and most widely known mood stabilizer is lithium, a natural mineral closely related to salt. For years, it was the only medication choice for people trying to cope with bipolar disorder. Although scientists have several theories about the overactive brain chemicals that lithium might target, they still don't know quite how the medication works—but it does seem to work. Lithium is one of the only medications that has high-quality evidence for reducing the risk of suicide. Unfortunately, while lithium can be very effective, the amount needed to help people feel better is close to a toxic dose. If you were on lithium, you would go for regular blood tests (every three months or less) to make sure your body was tolerating the medication. I took lithium safely for a long time, and it did a fair job at helping me stay stable. Personally, I thought the blood tests were a pain in the ass, but I got used to them. Aside from working well, lithium prescriptions (at least for generics) are cheap. Pharmaceutical companies have also developed extended-release versions (Eskalith, Lithobid).

Two other types of medications are currently used as mood stabilizers. One class of medications was originally designed to help people with seizures, and so they are called anticonvulsants. This group includes medications like divalproex (Depakote) and carbamazepine (Tegretol). Unfortunately, we don't have as much research on the effects of these medications for adolescents with bipolar disorder as we do for adults with the disorder. And as with lithium, we're not quite sure why anticonvulsants help regulate moods, but they might decrease neurotransmitter activity in brain cells that are overactive. After lithium, I switched to another medication which has worked out well for me in the long term.

Antipsychotics may also be prescribed to help stabilize your mood, as they have been found to have useful mood-stabilizing effects. In particular, your doctor might prescribe one of the newer antipsychotic medications like olanzapine (Zyprexa) if you were diagnosed with bipolar disorder.

Electroconvulsive Therapy: The Not-So-Shocking News

Medication and psychotherapy are the most common treatments for depression. However, electroconvulsive therapy (ECT) is another option that's occasionally used for the most severe cases of depression, where at least two medications have been tried without success or the symptoms are so urgent that there isn't time to wait for other treatments to work.

Studies have shown that ECT can indeed be quite helpful for many people with severe depression. Unfortunately, it is often referred to as "shock therapy," a misnomer that has helped give the therapy an undeserved bad rap in the public mind. In truth, the procedure isn't nearly as scary as its nickname makes it sound. In ECT, a carefully controlled electrical current is delivered to the brain, where it produces a brief seizure. This is thought to alter some of the electrical and chemical processes involved in brain functioning. A person receiving ECT is first given medication that keeps him or her from feeling pain and that prevents the body from convulsing. The seizure is contained within the brain, and it only lasts for about a minute. A few minutes later, the person awakens, just as someone would after minor surgery.

ECT usually consists of 6 to 12 such treatments, which are typically given three times a week. The effects appear gradually over the course of treatment, although they may be felt sooner than with medication and/or psychotherapy. The most common immediate side effects of ECT are headaches, muscle soreness, nausea, and confusion. Such effects generally clear up quickly. As the treatments go on, some people also develop problems with memory. While most of these problems clear up within days to months after the last ECT treatment, they occasionally last longer. On the flip side, some people say their memory is actually better after ECT, because their mind is no longer operating in a fog of depression.

Dealing with Side Effects

Much earlier in this book, I briefly talked about how various brain and body systems are intimately connected, and pointed out that cells can have different responses to the same chemical. Because of these two facts, medications (or herbs, street drugs, and so on) usually have some unintended effects. Sometimes this can be beneficial, as when an antidepressant that makes people drowsy ends up helping with insomnia. However, most of the time when we talk about side effects, we're referring to the ones that aren't so helpful.

Most of the time when we talk about side effects, we're referring to the ones that aren't so helpful.

Like the treatments that generate them, side effects can be classified in a number of ways. I think about side effects in terms of three factors: First, is a given side effect annoying or is it dangerous? Second, is it temporary or is it a chronic (ongoing) problem? Third, is it common or is it rare?

- *Annoying, common side effects that are temporary* include dry mouth, headaches, nausea, and diarrhea. In research studies, some people experience these types of side effects even when they are taking a fake medication (known as a placebo) that contains only a form of sugar. Most of these side effects are problems you've dealt with at some point in your life, and you can usually use whatever remedy worked for you last time. For dry mouth, which happens because your mouth isn't producing the amount of saliva that it normally does, the first thing you can do about it is to trust your instincts and drink more fluids, particularly water (but

What About Dietary Supplements?

Many people have tried dietary supplements as a way to treat the biological factors that play a role in mental health. You may have heard about this type of treatment, known as alternative medicine, especially for depression. Although there is only limited research evidence to support the claims that the manufacturers of various supplements make about their benefits, a few alternative treatments deserve mention here.

St. John's wort may be the most widely known herbal remedy for depression. Current research suggests that it may be useful for mild depression but not for moderate or severe symptoms of depression. Another natural compound, S-adenosyl-L-methionine (sold as SAM-e), has preliminary evidence for reducing the symptoms of depression, but the results are not yet conclusive. Fish oil (omega-3 fatty acids) has been shown to help relieve depression and stabilize mood.

Other types of herbal supplements have the potential to help people improve their mental health, but again, we don't have good research on which herbs work on which symptoms. You should also know that, like manufactured medications, naturally occurring chemicals (from herbs or minerals like lithium) could also have side effects. Additionally, herbal supplements are not regulated by the FDA. Thus, all herbal supplements are required to print the FDA disclaimer:

These statements and products have not been evaluated by the FDA. They are not intended to diagnose, treat, cure, or prevent any disease or condition. If you have a health concern or condition, consult a physician. Always consult a medical doctor before modifying your diet, using any new product, drug, supplement, or doing any new exercises.

In contrast, prescription medications are regulated by the FDA and backed by scientific studies as well as clinical experience.

If you want to explore the use of alternative herbal remedies to combat your mental health issues, *talk to your doctor first.* He or she will have useful information and advice about trying supplements like St. John's wort, and about the potential risks of doing so. For example, herbal supplements may have harmful interactions with drugs you're already taking. The bottom line? Again, you should work with your doctor to figure out the best combination of treatments for your health and well-being.

you might have to go to the restroom more often). You can also try things like gum, mints, or cough drops that make your mouth produce extra saliva. To keep your teeth healthy, you should choose sugarless products. For headaches, nausea, and diarrhea, try aspirin, ibuprofen (Advil), acetaminophen (Tylenol), and other over-the-counter medications.

• *Annoying, common side effects that become chronic issues* include weight gain (or weight loss), drowsiness, dizziness, restlessness, and sexual problems. You can cope with weight changes by using common strategies such as changing your diet, your exercise routine, and the amount of water that you drink. For the most part, drowsiness and dizziness may occur shortly after you take a dose of medication, so some people take their medication right before going to sleep. Most cases of restlessness that

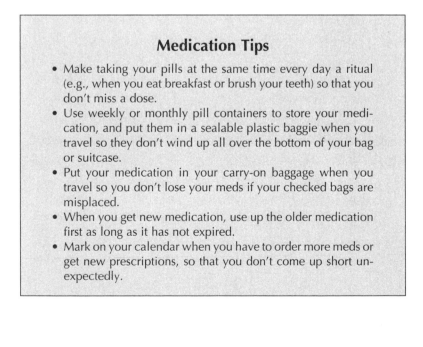

Medication Tips

• Make taking your pills at the same time every day a ritual (e.g., when you eat breakfast or brush your teeth) so that you don't miss a dose.
• Use weekly or monthly pill containers to store your medication, and put them in a sealable plastic baggie when you travel so they don't wind up all over the bottom of your bag or suitcase.
• Put your medication in your carry-on baggage when you travel so you don't lose your meds if your checked bags are misplaced.
• When you get new medication, use up the older medication first as long as it has not expired.
• Mark on your calendar when you have to order more meds or get new prescriptions, so that you don't come up short unexpectedly.

don't decrease on their own over time can be dealt with by adjusting the dose of medication. Some medications may cause such sexual side effects as reduced interest in sex, difficulty getting aroused, and difficulty reaching orgasm. Like restlessness, these problems often go away as your body adapts to the new medication. If they become chronic, you can work with your doctor to adjust the dose, add a medication that counteracts this effect, or try a different medication altogether.

• *Rare or dangerous side effects* include loss of muscle control, spasms of the tongue and jaw, increased anxiety or depression (see the box on pages 96 an 97), severe agitation, and strange rashes. If you experience any of these symptoms, you should report them to your doctor immediately. Most of the rare or dangerous side effects are medication-specific. Your doctor may request certain medical tests, sometimes on a regular basis, to make sure that you are not harmed by the medication. You should also be aware that sometimes side effects arise because of an interaction between medications (or herbs, alcohol, street drugs, or caffeine). That is why it is extremely important to tell your doctor about the other things you are taking, and about any recent changes in what you're taking.

Paying for Treatment

Most of the time, an insurance plan will cover the majority of treatment costs, although it may require that the patient give a relatively small co-pay for each visit to a health or mental health professional. In the United States, there are three major types of insurance. The first are plans, like Medicaid, that are sponsored by the federal or state government. Most teens and young adults don't get insurance through the government, although some young people under the age of 18 or those with severe psychiatric symptoms can get assistance; see more information about this below. A health maintenance organization (HMO) manages the second type of insurance. With an HMO, you can choose only from a particular list of providers to get coverage. Generally, the list of providers is extensive, but certain types of treatment may not be covered. The third type of insurance is the preferred provider organization (PPO). With a PPO, you have a list of "preferred providers" from whom you will get the maximum insurance coverage, but you can get some insurance reimbursement even if you go to a provider who is not on the list. There are many subtle differences between plans, even if they use the same major provider. Your insurance company can tell you more about what your plan does and does not cover.

Unfortunately, many (around 20% of) teens and young adults do not have any insurance coverage, but even with insurance, health care, and thus mental health care, can be expensive. If you have low income, little insurance, or no insurance, you still have some options:

- If you are under the age of 18 and your parents don't have insurance, you might qualify for services through Medicaid or the State Child Health Insurance Program (SCHIP). These are government programs that provide medical and mental health care to those who meet eligibility criteria. The programs vary from state to state. To find out what your state offers, start with Gov Benefits.gov (800–333–4636, www.govbenefits.gov) and Insure Kids Now! (877–543–7669, www.insurekidsnow.gov).

- Some communities (particularly those in urban centers) have community mental health centers that provide a range of mental health services at little or no cost. You can find the locations of these centers in the phone book or using an Internet search.
- Some therapists and psychiatrists can charge you based on a sliding scale, meaning they adjust the cost of each session based on your income.
- Just about all of the mutual-support groups are free.
- Many pharmaceutical companies sponsor Patient Assistance Programs that help people get medications (as well as vaccines and antibiotics) for free or at discount prices.
- The availability of generic medications also cuts down on the cost.

The Bottom Line

This was a long chapter, so you might be experiencing some information overload by now. Here's the main point I want you to take away: *There are many options for getting help.* You owe it to yourself to seriously consider other options before you decide that suicide is the only way out of your pain. I know it can be hard to think of alternatives, so talk them over with someone else, particularly a mental health professional.

> You owe it to yourself to seriously consider other options before you decide that suicide is the only way out of your pain.

You *can* get past this dark time in your life, and more importantly, you *can* have a life that you want to live.

Chapter Five

Recovery

I n my first session with Dr. O, I had promised to stay alive at
least until our next session the following week, and I fully
intended to keep my word. That did not mean, though, that I
immediately stopped thinking about suicide. In fact, you already know about some of what happened over the next few
weeks: the planning for my jump, the writing of my suicide
note, and the sending of those e-mails to friends, in which I
desperately tried to convince them that suicide was my best
option. I planned to kill myself on Friday, December 1. I had
an appointment with Dr. O. where I could fulfill my promise
to tell her before I died. It was also my brother's birthday,
which just seemed to complete the circle of life. Then on
Monday evening, November 27, 1995, Campus Police and
Security arrived to escort me out of the computer lab from
where I was sending those e-mails. I was taken to a nearby private psychiatric hospital the next day.

Hospital Log

November 28, 1995

They finally "came and got me" that night. "Mr. Lezine? Would you come with us?" they said. "A trip to Health Services," they said. They had come, and I knew they would. Yeah, I knew it.

My counselors were there, looking at my shame. "Couldn't handle it," they probably thought. "What the hell?" they surely wondered. I hid it pretty well. I had worn a mask—a very happy, almost stress-free mask. I had done it for years, never was that hard, but I had it removed that night. The question on everybody's mind except mine was "Why?" I knew why.

The question on everybody's mind except mine was "Why?" I knew why.

Campus police took me in a squad car, after escorting me through the building. They "escorted" me to the second floor of Health Services to talk to a psychologist. I closed the door and sat down, looking in that general direction, down.

She wanted me to see the Dean of Student Life. She thought I should consider a "Hospital." "I'm not hurt yet," I thought. "If I don't succeed Friday night, then yeah, sure a hospital would be needed." Not what she meant, though. Shot me with the idea of Quix being in a Mad House. Yeah, right.

I talked to my friends after I was cleared to go home. They took me back to the dorm in the squad car. They stole my dignity and robbed my pride. My friends said try "it," the Loony Bin. They said "it" might help, the Nut House. They said "it" might "cure" me, the Funny Farm. Yeah, right.

The next day I talked to the Dean. He said I was in danger of being kicked out of school for being a "burden to the University Services and placing others in a difficult situation."

"Sorry," thought I, "but I wasn't the one that called Police & Security, or you." I said I'd try a "Hospital," anything not to lose my beloved university. They couldn't take that from me, not after taking so much already. Hell, no. So, "Take me away. Lock me up," I said . . . basically, "Yes."

The Dean told me he wanted me to go to lunch with a friend as he set up my stay. They didn't trust me to go to lunch by myself, not even to lunch! He thought I might "change my mind." They smashed my dignity. I rode to the "Hospital" in a squad car. I'm getting used to being treated like a criminal. What? No handcuffs?

When I got to the hospital, I saw all the others, yeah . . . all of the other "nuts." The others who had "lost their marbles." Great. I had no self-respect. They told me to see the nurse who asked me questions, making me open up again. Getting used to that. Always the same, "Why do you want to kill yourself? What did you plan on doing,?" or that damned open-ended one, "So . . . what's been going on?"

Screw it! Fine. I opened up. Yeah . . . I should be here. Let me in if you think I do. Here's my case. She had me registered. They had me committed. It felt like I had just lost my soul. I had given it away so many times. This was my deepest secret, my personal ideal for a private death. I gave it away, all of the damn details: the 8-story parking garage with open access that I could describe very well, considering the extent of planning, the suicide note sealed with my heart and pain. I gave it all to complete and total strangers over and over again. "Share your soul."

What was there left to do? I couldn't even cry . . . no clothes, no change of underwear, no music, nothing but me. I was considered a risk to myself. I was on 5-minute checks. I ate. I slept.

November 29, 1995

First day in full in this place. They sucked some blood from my veins for their blood test and then took a urine sample before checking my vital signs. I grabbed some Cap'n Crunch, a bowl, a nicely rounded plastic spoon, and low fat milk. Not bad.

I saw my doctor . . . who was a kind, elderly lady and the intern who was with her, name slips the mind. Anyhow, the doctor asked the questions and the intern scribbled away, notes on technique, approach, tidbits of my behind-the-scenes struggle. She put me on Zoloft, an antidepressant with few side effects. Yeah, drugs . . . okay, prescription medication, whatever.

I had a Recreation Group, and played a game. Here, in the middle of Final Exams, I was playing a game of Taboo. Unbelievable. Did some good, though, probably. We also made snowflakes from paper. Outside, it snowed. Two days ago, Toni asked me where I was. I said hell. They'd get me into the Crazy House when hell froze. Guess what? Hell froze. Ha ha. So there I was making paper snowflakes with the other nuts. They were people like any others, people with problems, with medical and psychological difficulties. They were people who had been pushed to the edge of life and were here. We had all been at an edge, that's why we were here. We were trying to live in such a messed up world, with inherent illnesses, and few coping skills. We got screwed. It wasn't something to be ashamed of . . . we never had much control to begin with.

November 30, 1995

Basically I was feeling good . . . about ready to get out, to "fly the coop," to "make haste." Any more time in this place will drive me insane. My mind was clear. I knew I had a lot to work on, but that would need time, it wasn't happening here. I had served my time.

December 1, 1995, Friday

I informed my doctor that I was ready to flee from the Mad House. She asked me some questions, you know, the usual, "How are you feeling today? Do you still want to kill yourself? Are you ready to go back to school?" I answered. I was ready to leave the hospital.

I went to Psychological Services and met with the Head Psych. She asked me some questions, you know, the usual soul-searching, bear-your-thoughts-and-feelings, unveil-your-darkest-secrets-to-a-complete-stranger type questions. I answered. I was ready to leave the hospital.

I saw the Dean, and he said the first concern was whether or not I was going to hurt myself. That was fine. He said he didn't want me placing any "burdens" on University Services or other students. I said, "Fine." What a stupid thing for him to say! Let's say I was still suicidal but good at covering it up. [Before] I told my close friends I was going to kill myself, and they called to have me placed under protective custody. I did what I had to do. [But now] it was Friday, my guarantee was over. I [could] go to the top of the parking garage, call to somebody below. He/she runs up or gets someone to come up. I tell them, "Here's my suicide note. See this gets into the right hands." I jump. See? I wouldn't have contacted anybody or disturbed or "burdened" University Services. I would have just died. I ask anyone reading this, would it be better for a suicidal person to say something to someone although it might disturb them, or to commit a silent death? Which are they encouraging? That's just not right.

Anyhow, here I am, sitting in the hospital. My roommate knows I'm here. I don't know what to expect from dorm mates. I need to come to grips with the years of silent pain I've suffered. It will be very painful. It has already been so. I think, though, that sometimes a wound needs to be opened and the poison sucked out before it can heal properly. I am opening my wounds, and it hurts like hell, but I am going to heal and I am going to be a stronger person as a result.

Everybody probably thinks I'm a nut. That's all right because I guess I am. They'll pass me from doctor to doctor for the rest of my life. Everyone gets a try at the nut. Pass him along. Nobody could love me, only pity me. They'll say, "Poor guy lost his mind." Nobody will ever look up to me again. I have fallen from the pedestal!! I have fallen from grace. I was a hero once, a role model. I was someone, maybe not much of a someone inside, maybe just a shell, but something. It was all I knew and I lost it, and with it I've lost me. Now everybody cares, and everyone wants to help me. "Let me support you," they say. Everybody is worried. That was me before, dammit! That was me. I did the supporting.

> I am opening my wounds, and it hurts like hell, but I am going to heal and I am going to be a stronger person as a result.

The Immediate Aftermath of a Suicidal Crisis

My suicidal crisis landed me in a psychiatric hospital, but if a person is discovered to have made a suicide attempt, he or she is usually brought first to a hospital emergency room. On the way to the hospital, paramedics or an emergency medical technician (EMT) might perform CPR or administer first aid and medications to keep the person alive. If the person has taken an overdose, the doctors at the hospital might give him or her charcoal (activated carbon) to drink because it forms strong connections to other drugs in the stomach, thus preventing the body from absorbing those drugs. A brownish-black sludge, the substance is basically the same as what we use in water filters and fish tanks. Sometimes charcoal is not enough, though, and the doctors might have to pump everything out of the stomach. They slide a tube through the mouth or nose and guide it down to the stomach, and then slowly siphon out the fluid.

Someone who enters the hospital unconscious, intoxicated, or otherwise unable to breathe properly may have to be intubated. In the intubation procedure, a health professional places a flexible plastic tube into the throat to assist with artificial breathing techniques. Whether or not someone requires intubation, he or she might then be treated in other areas of the hospital besides the emergency department, like trauma surgery or the intensive care unit (ICU).

Once a person is medically stabilized, he or she will likely undergo a psychiatric evaluation and possibly be referred to a psychiatric hospital. If alcohol or street drugs are involved, the person may go to a detoxification center first so that the substance can be cleared out of his or her system.

Psychiatric hospitals usually include psychiatrists, psychiatric nurses, psychologists, social workers, and psychiatric technicians. At teaching hospitals, which are affiliated with medical schools or psychology departments at universities, there may also be mental health professionals who under the supervision of senior staff are finishing their training—interns, residents, and fellows. If you end up in a hospital that is well staffed, you could expect individual therapy, group therapy, and consultation with a psychiatrist and perhaps a social worker. Unfortunately, many hospitals are not well staffed. You can at least expect to meet with a psychiatrist and have staff around 24 hours a day to see how you're responding to treatment and to make sure you're safe.

Like me, many people who enter the hospital after a suicidal crisis are placed on some type of suicide watch. While on watch, I couldn't have belts, shoelaces, headphones (with a cord), shavers, or anything else that could conceivably be dangerous. People on staff brought meals to me in the unit because they couldn't trust me to go down to the cafeteria with the others. Someone had to look in on me about every 5 minutes. I understand the precautions, but let me tell you that it is hard to sleep when somebody comes along and opens the door every 5 to 10 minutes.

I was in a psychiatric hospital for a few days, and I have done everything in my power never to have to go back. It provides intensive mental health care in a safe environment, but you can't achieve your goals in life while you're in a hospital, and I suddenly felt I had too much to do. I have seen some people go in and out of the hospital in crisis after crisis. I have seen others shuffled from hospitals to jails or prisons, and then back to the hospital. I have even seen people who have been in the hospital for years—so long that they have forgotten what it is like to be on the outside. Having seen many types of hospitals from the perspective of patient and professional, here's my advice: Use the hospital as a short-term option for help in getting through a suicidal crisis, but then get back to your life as soon as possible. You may also look into finding a program that lies somewhere in between full hospitalization and weekly therapist appointments: *Day treatment,* or *partial hospitalization,* is an option in which people continue intensive mental health care during the day but go home in the evenings and on weekends.

I firmly believe that no matter what your situation is, you can always take some small step that gets you closer to your goals. Work with your treatment team (your psychiatrist, therapist, and any others who are treating you) to find a way to get through the crisis, and then move past it. My very first goals during my hospital stay were quite simple: Get off suicide watch, get my CD player back, and earn enough staff trust to be allowed to go down to the cafeteria with everyone else. Eventually, I moved on to the next goals: Get out of the hospital, and then stay out of the hospital.

Eventually, I moved on to the next goals: Get out of the hospital, and then stay out of the hospital.

The Road to Recovery

With a deep breath, I walked through the outer doors of the hospital on Saturday, December 2, 1995. The bus didn't run as often on Saturdays, so I walked along the winding road that separated the psychiatric hospital from the outside world. The crisp winter air felt good; it was as if I could smell the freedom. I put on my headphones, cranked up the volume on my CD player, and walked. Final exams were far from my mind. I made a silent promise to everyone I had left behind on the ward: *I will not forget, and the college has no idea about the hell I am going to start as a mental health advocate.* I entered the hospital feeling depressed and defeated, but I left with a fiery defiance. Maybe I was trying to find some meaning in all of the pain and humiliation of my suicidal experience. Maybe I had reconnected with the fighter in me called Alexander, and the idealist called Quix. Whatever it was, I wanted to make my life better.

And yet, it was a rough start—I still wasn't functioning at 100%. I ended the semester on academic probation, and I was emotionally fragile. My therapist wrote the following summary of my state after our last session of the semester:

> He is very concerned about what his parents' reaction will be. He is also concerned about having destroyed the image of the reliable, competent, helpful young man . . . part of him feels relieved because he then can be supported and taken care of. Another part . . . is grieving and mourning the fact that he doesn't have that image any more after he was hospitalized. He is hopeless about his family's reaction to the pain. . . . He has never been accustomed to hearing his parents being supportive and nurturing toward him. . . .

When I returned home to California, I was crushed by the harsh or negative reactions I got from people there. Their attitude nearly pushed me off track. My dad didn't really understand what was happening to his son, and my psychiatrist was recommending further hospitalization. Dad didn't trust the hospitals, which had done little for others in our family, and he gave me the choice. I decided to go back to college; that place wasn't going to get rid of me that easily. My father supported my decision. After all, he had named me Alexander for a reason.

Was it all smooth-going from then on? Hardly. The road to recovery from a suicidal crisis is rocky at first, and all that

The road to recovery from a suicidal crisis is rocky at first, and all that precipitated that crisis doesn't just suddenly go away once you've resolved to get your life back on track.

precipitated that crisis doesn't just suddenly go away once you've resolved to get your life back on track. That resolve is critically important, though—a huge step in the right direction—and you'll need to remind yourself of it constantly as, with help, you face your demons, understand where they come from, and learn how to manage or overcome them. Your resolve will help you face other problems as well, depending on your own particular circumstances and those the world throws in your way.

Dealing with the Physical Scars

First of all, let's talk about the physical consequences of suicide attempts and other types of self-injury. Lethal or violent suicide attempts damage the body or can leave one with terrible scars. Whether or not someone intends to die by cutting, burning, or other self-inflicted injury, these methods can leave permanent marks. Many people try to hide their scars under long sleeve shirts or turtlenecks, but even then, they often worry about others discovering their secret. Other people may show no visible signs of injury, but suffer from internal organ damage from drug overdoses or chronic use of chemicals.

I don't want to leave you thinking that the situation is hopeless, though. The human body can be remarkably resilient, as can the human brain, when we cooperate with the inborn desire to live. With a combination of medical treatment, physical therapy, time, and a lot of hard work, many people can recover much of their functioning. I've said that suicidal behavior is incredibly complex, so it makes sense that recovery, including recovery of physical function, will take time, too. Doctors, therapists, hospitals, and medications are all helpful, but nothing is a quick fix or a cure. You have to want to get better. You have to follow up on the options for finding a better life. If you invest in your own future, then recovery is possible.

Dealing with Stigma

Aside from the physical effects, there are social consequences of a suicide attempt. I just alluded to this consequence in my own story. I had good reasons to worry about what family and friends would think after they learned about what had happened. Most people are scared, and in an effort to protect themselves from even having to think about such a thing as suicide, they may push us away. I couldn't list all the friends, and family of friends, who stopped talking to me once they learned of my attempt. Many people in my religious congregation wouldn't visit me or talk to me anymore. Those who don't push us away might still treat us differently after a suicide attempt. I had to get used to parents and friends always asking, "Are you doing okay?" or "Are you taking your meds?" (Okay, so I still haven't completely gotten used to that.)

People will come up with all kinds of reasons to explain their behavior, like the notion that suicidal feelings are contagious; that suicidal people might become violent or start behaving badly; that people with a mental illness can't be trusted; or that mental illness makes people incompetent. In the world of mental health, this effect is called *stigma*. In ancient Greece, a stigma was a kind of tattoo that was cut or burned into the skin of criminals, slaves, traitors, and other people who were to be avoided and shunned by the public. Many groups have faced stigma and discrimination at some time, including people who are left-handed, gay or lesbian, racial or ethnic minorities, blind, deaf, paralyzed, or living with HIV/AIDS or other diseases. At least in the United States, there also continues to be stigma attached to suicidal acts and to mental illness. It is so pervasive that it is part of our culture.

But stigma isn't exclusive to the general public. Some of the discrimination I've faced as a result of being open about my suicide crisis has come from psychiatrists, psychologists, and even professionals who specialize in suicide prevention. I've had professors tell me that I shouldn't have mentioned my past in my applications to Ph.D. programs, and I've had doctors treat my suffering dismissively as a "suicidal gesture" or a "failed suicide attempt." People who attempt suicide or experience psychiatric symptoms might even stigmatize themselves. Between the stigma that makes us question our own worth and the fear of having others "discover" our condition, many people avoid getting mental health care. Honestly, the shame I endured hurt like hell. Still, I got the help I needed to get on with my life (with or without the people who doubted me). It does get easier as you go along, and as you find out who your true friends are and who you can rely on during difficult times.

Getting Back on Your Feet

Previously I said that my suicidal crisis was like a tsunami that overwhelmed me, knocking me over and pounding the life right out of me. Thinking about the entire story, though, I now think that maybe it was more like an earthquake. Just when I realized that I'd survived the initial quake and started surveying the damage, there were all these aftershocks. It felt like my entire world had become unstable. Everything I had taken for granted had to be renovated, if not demolished and reconstructed altogether. In addition to getting professional treatment, including medication and psychotherapy, I can think of five other things that helped me to re-

Everything I had taken for granted had to be renovated, if not demolished and reconstructed altogether.

build my life. I'm sure you can come up with an even better list for yourself, but this might give you some ideas to start with.

IDEA #1: BUILD A SUPPORT NETWORK

For some of us, particularly introverts like me, this idea remains easier said than done. However, just in case I haven't already made this concept abundantly clear, research consistently shows that social support can help people feel less suicidal and generally happier with life. You could start by building on (or improving) the relationships with your close friends and family. Maybe they could introduce you to other people or accompany you when you go out for some social occasion. Generally, when I attend a party or gathering with someone I already know, I feel more comfortable about mingling and meeting new people. I know that, no matter what, I will at least have someone there that I can talk to. If you're not into going to social events or parties, then start with whatever type of communication you are most comfortable with (like text messaging, instant messaging, phone calls, or e-mail). Some people have found supportive communities through the Internet, using sites like MySpace or Facebook. The main caution about the Internet is that it is so open that just about anyone can put up a Web site and say whatever they want, including sex offenders, ex-cons, con artists, and other shady characters. Remember, the idea here is to find people who can support your efforts to build a healthy life. Whatever you do, online or in person, I think you'll

... the idea here is to find people who can support your efforts to build a healthy life.

be better off if it is in line with your life goals, and not based on a momentary impulse or pressure from someone else.

IDEA #2: FIND ENJOYABLE ACTIVITIES

Identify two or three things that you really enjoy doing and schedule a regular time each week to do them. Think about what you would do if you had millions of dollars and all the time in the day that you wanted to spend them. In other words, I'm not referring to activities that you do because you get something in return (like money), but rather to the activities that you enjoy just for the thrill of doing them. In cognitive-behavioral therapy, the therapist almost always recommends such activities, and for good reason: You're likely to feel better as a result of pursuing them. That sounds obvious, I'm sure, but it's a point worth emphasizing. We often stop doing what we truly enjoy when we're depressed, or when we get too caught up in what "needs to get done" or what "should get done." I know I'm guilty of letting this slip sometimes. I used to love to draw, and I had a regular comic strip in our college newspaper. Now I hardly ever draw, and I keep telling myself that one day, "when I have more time," I'll get back to drawing. Nobody's perfect. I do, however, still play video games as an emotional outlet, and I try to watch a movie or go for a walk a few times each week.

IDEA #3: GET SOME SLEEP

We all have times when we really need to get something done, working late into the night (probably because we were procrastinating), or when we just can't get to sleep. When I was in high school and college, I'd stay up until all hours of the night, sometimes pulling all-nighters to get a project done. When you or your friends are in class during the day, it is tempting to do things together in the evening or at night, but there's a price to pay for not getting enough sleep. When we sleep, our body has time to heal itself, restore balance to the brain and organs, and consolidate our memories. If you don't get enough sleep, you are more likely to get sick and to take longer to recover from even common illnesses like the cold or flu. People who do not get enough sleep (especially through chronic sleep deprivation) tend to have difficulty keeping their emotions stable, and become more irritable, hyper, depressed, or anxious (maybe even paranoid). It is also harder to remember things and harder to concentrate (counteracting the goal of all-night study sessions). Sleep is a natural part of life for humans, animals, and even ants or flies, because it is a survival function. Try to get into a regular sleep pattern, and be consistent about when you go to sleep and when you wake in the morning. It is easier to have a stable mind when you have a stable routine.

Idea #4: Exercise

In college I played club sports like basketball and went on long walks, then in graduate school I took up Aikido (a martial art). Besides helping us look and feel more physically fit, exercise can help lower blood pressure, improve sleep, and lift mild depression. Some people feel good during moderate to vigorous exercise because the activity makes the body release endorphins (called *opioid peptides*). These natural opioids, like the drugs that try to mimic their effect, induce positive, slightly euphoric feelings—the original natural high. Vigorous exercise

> *Besides helping us look and feel more physically fit, exercise can help lower blood pressure, improve sleep, and lift mild depression.*

includes jogging, climbing stairs, aerobics, spinning or cycling, swimming, and many martial arts. Some people prefer low-impact exercise that emphasizes deep breathing and stretching, like yoga, pilates, or tai chi. In the long term, regular exercise can increase blood and oxygen flow to your brain, promoting better thinking and mental health. If you exercise with other people, you get a two-for-one: the additional source of social support. For example, my Aikido group was an essential source of support for me as I completed graduate school. Even if you exercise alone, it can be a great way to work off pent-up emotions. I couldn't count the number of times that a long walk helped me calm down enough to deal with some stressful situation.

Idea #5: Volunteer

Through high school and college, I enjoyed volunteering in various ways. Early on, I tutored students who were struggling in classes and helped peers with college applications. In college, I found my calling in suicide prevention. Some people enjoy becoming a Big Brother or Big Sister, or being a mentor through a similar program. Other people make time to volunteer at an elderly home, soup kitchen, shelter, or neighborhood organization. Research shows that people who volunteer generally have better well-being and may be less depressed. I enjoy feeling like I might be helping someone else, and others have reported that this altruism improves their mood as well. You also have the opportunity to be engaged in some meaningful activity (possibly doubling as an enjoyable activity) that could provide another source of social support.

What if You Start to Feel Suicidal Again?

It would be great if I could tell you that I had "seven keys" or "tricks" to never feeling suicidal again. I wish I could tell you that once you get past a suicidal crisis, you are done and you can put the issue behind you. I would be lying, though, and I promised not to do that. Maybe some people have a single suicidal crisis and never deal with it again, at least as far as we know. However, for many of us, some stressful situation or resurgence of symptoms will trigger the painfully familiar thoughts of death. If we follow through on our treatment and work at recovery, then we can reduce the frequency and intensity of suicidal thoughts. Yet sometimes they break through anyhow. What then? That is when you need to do everything possible to prevent an important person from dying: you. To me, that is the most important form of suicide prevention.

As I have said before, coping with something as big as the life-or-death decision of suicide calls for a second (and third, fourth, fifth . . .) opinion. Talk to someone that you are close to, and consult with a mental health professional. If you have a psychiatrist or therapist, then call him or her, no matter what time it is or whether they're expecting your call. If you're not in treatment right now, but there is someone whom you used to see for mental health care, then call that person. Don't believe that he or she will be disappointed or upset. For a mental health professional, nothing can compare to the devastation of losing a client to suicide. If you have to, then page the therapist or doctor, but make contact as soon as possible. If you can't reach someone, or can't bring yourself to call someone you know, then call the National Suicide Prevention Lifeline (1-800-273-TALK). You will automatically be routed to a crisis call center in your area so that staff

If you can't reach someone, or can't bring yourself to call someone you know, then call the National Suicide Prevention Lifeline (1-800-273-TALK).

there can help you identify some local resources. If you feel like you just can't hold back, that the suicidal urge is just too strong, then call 911 or go to the emergency department.

Sometimes we might not feel like we're on the verge of attempting suicide, but we just can't shake the painful feelings that lead up to suicidal thoughts. There are some things that you can do for yourself to get through the suicidal crisis. The best coping strategies may be the ones that have worked for you in the past. Again, your list is going to be better than mine, but I can offer a few suggestions to get you started.

COPING STRATEGY #1: DISTRACTION

Suicidal or depressed thoughts tend to feed off of one another, creating a vortex that sucks you down into despair. Such brooding or ruminating makes the suicidal urge stronger. Sometimes I've been able to break this chain of events by finding a way to take a time-out from the crisis and think about something completely different. It can be hard to take your mind off of serious problems, so it helps to use techniques that foster positive emotions. Laughter and joy don't mix with sadness and gloom—it's like trying to squat and jump at the same time. For me, the easiest way to take my mind off my troubles is to watch a funny or uplifting movie. The effect of a comedy can be amplified by watching it with other people, even if you go out to a theater by yourself, because the laughter of others around you can be infectious. The unconditional love and happiness offered by a pet (particularly a dog or cat) can have similarly uplifting effects. Some hospitals have taken advantage of this fact by implementing Animal Assisted Therapy programs.

There are other ways to refocus on positive things as well. Memories that are associated with emotions are generally easier to recall, partially because we have a special part of the brain (the amygdala) that specializes in emotional memories. When we feel depressed, it is easier to remember negative or depressing events in our past (like rejections, failures, pain, and loss); this condition is known as *state-dependent recall.* This process can work in the opposite direction as well: Positive memories can activate positive emotions. I have a collection of pictures and letters that remind me of good memories, or of what I've done well in the past (e.g., thank you cards, get well cards, letters from friends, pictures of award ceremonies). When I'm feeling down, I can pull out this collection and remember that life hasn't been 100% bad. It should be even easier to create, and find, a digital folder with similar content. For me, certain songs also remind me of events or sentiments that can counteract depressed feelings. Some of the songs were popular during times when I was doing well, so they remind me of those times. Other songs have lyrics that I can identify with, like "Mad Season" and "Unwell" by Matchbox 20, or sentiments that I identify with, like "Fighter" by Christina Aguilera and "Die Another Day" by Madonna. I've made mp3 playlists and CDs that start off with songs that mirror my angry or depressed feeling and progressively change to ones that reassure me that I can make it through another day. You know best what makes you think about good things from the past—a picture, a letter, a song, a place, a taste, a smell—and you can use that knowledge of yourself to create your own collection of positive associations.

You know best what makes you think about good things from the past—a picture, a letter, a song, a place, a taste, a smell—and you can use that knowledge of yourself to create your own collection of positive associations.

COPING STRATEGY #2: PERSPECTIVE

When something happens that seems so devastating that someone considers suicide, it tends to grab the spotlight and push everything else in life into the periphery. It can be helpful to put everything in perspective and remember the big picture. First, though, it is important to acknowledge your pain—I'm not trying to say that the painful circumstance is insignificant. On the contrary, when something upsetting happens to me, I like to write about it. Then I really examine it. How long is this problem likely to last? Have I dealt with this before, and if so, then how did I get through it last time? I try to remind myself that no matter how much pain I'm in, even if it feels like things will never get better, my agony probably won't last forever. Most of the time I can say to myself, *I have been through worse than this,* or at least *I have suffered through this before.* When you've lived through a suicidal crisis, you can remind yourself of that accomplishment: You *have* successfully made it through this before.

At one point I considered suicide as a form of revenge: *when I'm dead, they'll be sorry.* I was angry at someone else and channeling that rage into thoughts of my own death. We think about revenge when we're hurt. Sometimes we don't acknowledge our own pain, instead moving straight to thinking of ways to hurt the other person. When I thought about it later, it didn't make sense—I felt hurt, and my response was to hurt or kill *myself?* When we're hurt, shouldn't we try to soothe the pain and to heal? If you are hurt badly, then the most important thing is to find a way to make yourself feel better. There are many ways to accomplish this goal, and hurting yourself is not one of them. After you take care of yourself, you can figure out how to avoid or deal with a similar painful situation in the future. By working on making yourself better, smarter, and stronger, you will also be building status and self-respect. Stated another way, I think the best revenge of all is living a fulfilled and useful life.

In terms of a time perspective, I try to imagine myself ten years from now and start with this question: "Honestly, will I feel as strongly about this problem in ten years?" Most of the time, the situation that causes such intense pain is only temporary. On the other hand, what *is* worth living for? What worthwhile or enjoyable things *could* you see or do or accomplish or experience in the next ten years? What are the *possibilities?* This is where someone from your support network can be invaluable. They can help you think about the possibility of you having a positive future. Find someone who can cheer you on, no matter what the odds are. Find someone who won't stop believing in you. Although my friend Amanda has passed away, I can still hear her saying, "I believe in you." I know that she would never want any harm to come to me, especially not self-inflicted injury or death. She kept telling me that she held a firm belief that I had a future worth living for. At times I was carried to the next day on the strength of her conviction.

> *I try to imagine myself ten years from now and start with this question: "Honestly, will I feel as strongly about this problem in ten years?"*

COPING STRATEGY #3: PROBLEM SOLVING
It can be difficult to really think through a problem when we're in pain, so distraction can help initially. Sometimes the issue will resolve itself, or the problem is completely out of our hands and we just have to cope with it by looking at it within a larger context. Other times, we can do something about the problem, or at least prevent it from coming up again.

Cognitive-behavioral therapy or problem-solving therapy can help identify specific approaches to problems that work best for you.

You can start with the following general problem-solving strategy. The first task in solving an overwhelming problem is usually to break it up into smaller, specific problems. There are various ways to approach this task, but I like the visual approach. You start by writing down the primary problem, then you draw lines to factors that could be contributing to the problem (secondary issues).

> The first task in solving an overwhelming problem is usually to break it up into smaller, specific problems.

Ask yourself what could possibly be creating this problem or making it worse or stopping it from getting better. Next, you do the same process for each of the secondary issues. You can continue this process until you're listing issues that you feel comfortable tackling. Your next question might be, "With all of these smaller problems, where do I start?" As you look over your list, you'll see that some solutions will probably have a bigger effect, or take you closer to your goal, when compared to others. I rank my solutions in terms of how much impact each one will have. Then I start with the top-ranked solution that I am most comfortable with. Sometimes I get frustrated with working on small issues, because I want to solve my problem *now*. I have to remind myself that, as they say in Alcoholics Anonymous, I have to take it "one day at a time." Or, if you prefer, Confucius says, "The man who moves a mountain begins by carrying away small stones."

Many of my problems have involved some conflict with other people, and I doubt that I'm alone in that respect. There are entire books and classes devoted to the topic of dealing with interpersonal conflict situations. In fact, interpersonal therapy has been effective at addressing depression because it focuses on the social issues that can cause us so much pain. If you're having interpersonal problems, then I would strongly suggest that you look into the resources for dealing with conflict, and get advice that is more extensive and specific than I can provide here. However, I can offer several tips on strategies that I use to deal with interpersonal conflict. Most conflict situations, or their resolution, involve some type of communication, so we need to learn how to communicate effectively.

- *Identify the real problem:* Sometimes people argue about things that have already happened between them, or that they can't change. It can be helpful to focus on the facts of a situation and work together to find some solution. As a silly example, if we were roommates and the dishes were piling up in the sink, I could say something accusing like, "Why haven't you done the dishes?"—which would probably start an argument. Alternatively, I could talk to you about the problem (the dishes need to be cleaned), and we could work out how to resolve the situation (doing the dishes together, taking turns, and so on).
- *Use "I" statements:* In arguments and emotional situations, it can be easy to blame others for whatever is going wrong. However, when we say something blaming (even if it is true), the other person is likely to feel defensive and argumentative. This hardly ever solves the problem. So what is an "I statement"? Instead of saying, "You're wrong," you might say, "I see the problem differently." Instead of saying, "You make me mad," you would say, "I get really angry when you. . . ."

It is an honest way of telling the other person what you're thinking or feeling without putting them on the defensive.

- *Active listening:* When there is conflict, we tend to cling tenaciously to our own point of view, perhaps screening out just about everything the other person is saying as we think about what we're going to say next. However, I've found that I can take the steam out of many arguments quickly by listening carefully to what the other person is saying, and then acknowledging his or her feelings and perspective. The person is then much more likely to repay the favor by listening to my perspective.

- *Assertiveness:* When you are assertive, you can communicate your thoughts and feelings honestly and appropriately. I had a really tough time with assertiveness, hardly ever saying no to a request, and quietly suffered many unfair situations in which one individual or another took advantage of me. I've gotten better, but I'd still like to improve in this area. Lack of assertiveness is closely related to low self-esteem, so it shouldn't come as a surprise that many suicidal people have struggled with this issue. You should also realize that since low self-esteem develops over our lifetimes, it takes time to improve it. Identify opportunities to stand up for yourself, because by doing so you can raise your self-esteem. The goal of assertiveness is to be able to tell others about your thoughts, feelings, needs, or wants in an appropriate way that isn't aggressive or attacking.

The goal of assertiveness is to be able to tell others about your thoughts, feelings, needs, or wants in an appropriate way that isn't aggressive or attacking.

- *How you communicate:* Aside from the words that we use when communicating with others, facial expression, body language, and tone of voice also play into inter-personal conflict. Now that we've covered some ways to state what we want to say, the next step is making sure that everything else is in sync with the assertive stance. At one extreme, it is difficult to get past conflict if your tone of voice is tense or angry, if you scowl, if you cross your arms, if you point at the other person, or if you seem threatening in any way. At the other extreme, your thoughts and feelings might not be taken seriously if you are avoiding eye contact, shrinking back, speaking quietly, or otherwise indicating that you are not intent on standing up for yourself. I've found that it is quite effective to take a deep breath (or a few) before responding to someone. I try to maintain eye contact, without having an intense glare. If I'm nervous but trying not to show it, then I look at the person's nose or forehead, because he or she can't tell the difference. If I'm standing, then I try to stand with my feet about shoulder-width apart, a firm foundation. When it is my turn to speak, I try to speak at a normal pace, with the same vocal tone and volume that I would use if I was reading something out loud. The resulting effect is a good blend of exhibiting confidence in myself and showing respect for the other person.

I wish I could provide more specific advice, because dealing with conflict is one of the hardest challenges that we face. However, there are some excellent self-help and professional resources that are available to assist you with finding better ways to deal with conflict and to work through other problems as well. Some self-help information on these topics can be found on the Internet, such as the Wellness Recovery Action Plan site (*www.mentalhealthrecovery.com*). Books on conflict resolution can be found in the self-help or psychology sections of bookstores or libraries. Many therapists can also help you learn or practice methods for solving problems and dealing with conflicts.

Moving Forward and Building Mental Health

People generally tend to focus more on negatives than on positives. If you think about the comments in red ink on class papers, or about the stories that are highlighted in the daily news, then I'm sure you know what I mean. Similarly, in mental health and suicide prevention, we have tended to focus on symptoms of mental illness and suicide risk, as opposed to focusing on the *health* in mental health. Of course, we're not alone; most health care is actually about illness, disease, and injury. However, there is a growing trend among some mental health professionals, as part of a new discipline called *positive psychology*, toward promoting positive mental health in young people (a movement known as *positive youth development*) and throughout the life course. While throughout this book I have tried to integrate some of the ideas that this trend has generated, they deserve special mention here.

After we get past our suicidal crisis, the goals of recovery should shift from basic survival to regaining a more complete sense of ourselves and to building a future we can look forward to.

After we get past our suicidal crisis, the goals of recovery should shift from basic survival to regaining a more complete sense of ourselves and to building a future we can look forward to.

Of course, it is important for us to treat symptoms and deal with stress, but we also need to acknowledge our talents, strengths, assets, interests, goals, and future potential. In Aikido, my instructor constantly reminds us not to focus on what part of us an attacker has grabbed a hold of, but to think about all the possibilities that are left with the body parts that are free. We need to approach life with a similar perspective, especially when we have been wrestling with something as powerful as a suicidal crisis.

To successfully regain a sense of control over your life and to reach your goals, you will need to have both the ability (skills) to achieve them and the *perception* that you have that ability or that you can enhance your ability (self-efficacy). The types of abilities I'm referring to include being able to communicate and work well with others, to identify and understand emotions, to think and reason about issues, to take effective action steps, and to balance between your own rights and the rights of others. Sometimes we need to improve one or more of these abilities to reach a particular goal. You can take advantage of your various assets (personal strengths, supportive relationships, and available opportunities) to enhance these skills.

Some communities or organizations have started providing programs that help young people to develop positive skills or to build self-confidence and self-efficacy. Research shows that these types of programs can help improve coping ability, learning and school performance, decision making, and relationships with family and friends. In addition to encouraging positive development, such programs show evidence of reducing loneliness, anxiety, depression, and alcohol or drug abuse. Preliminary evidence also suggests that this type of positive prevention might help young people avoid having a suicidal crisis (or another one). The best programs provide numerous opportunities to engage teens and young adults in structured, age-appropriate activities that include supportive relationships. Many of the programs that have been developed are for high school (secondary school) or college students. However, there are some community-based programs for mentoring (like Big Brothers and Big Sisters) or activities at a community center.

I'm sure by now you've noticed that there are things that I continue to work on to improve my mental health and well-being. Even after ten years in suicide prevention and a Ph.D. in psychology, I still find it beneficial to listen to self-help recordings about self-esteem, read books on assertiveness, or play relaxation CDs. My medication helps me manage my symptoms pretty well, but there is more to life than dealing with psychiatric symptoms. Like me, you'll also find out that as you go through different stages of life, there are always new issues to contend with. There are new opportunities for growth as well, and that's what I really want you to realize. You deserve more than an existence spent simply avoiding a self-imposed death penalty (suicide); you deserve to *enjoy* life.

You deserve more than an existence spent simply avoiding a self-imposed death penalty (suicide); you deserve to enjoy life.

Chapter Six

Finding the Phoenix:
Where I Am Today

Imagine a beautiful and majestic bird that looks like a cross between a peacock and an eagle. Its feathers have the most brilliant reds and pure golds that you have ever seen. As you approach cautiously, you notice that the bird looks incredibly sad. You peer into its eyes, and it is as if they are telling you, "I am ugly, old, and wounded beyond recovery." In some ways, this seems unbelievable. How could such a remarkable bird seem so hopeless? In other ways, it seems all too familiar. Not long ago you may have felt the same way, or maybe you knew someone who suffered that way. Suddenly, the bird lights itself on fire. Although you try to rescue it, the bird is engulfed in flames, and soon it seems like there is nothing but ashes left. Some people would give up on the bird at this point. Not you. You decide to stay. Then something stirs in the charred nest. Looking closer, you see a baby bird pushing through the smoky ash. Then you notice that, although it is covered in gray and black dust, the little hatchling has feathers with the most brilliant reds and pure golds that you have ever seen. You have discovered a phoenix.

In ancient mythology, the phoenix would consume itself in fire if it believed that life was over, or if it had been wounded. The mythical bird would then be reborn from the ashes. Maybe you have heard about the phoenix from Harry Potter books, or X-Men comics, or some other story. The symbolism of the phoenix has been harnessed for centuries to represent a rebirth after catastrophe: on the flags of captains during the Greek Revolution; on the seal of San Francisco, California, after the devastating 1906 earthquake; on the seal of Atlanta, Georgia, after the city was burned on several occasions. Remember, though, that in the original myth, the phoenix burns itself—a suicidal act. Thus, it is even more fitting for the phoenix to represent our stories.

The symbolism of the phoenix has been harnessed for centuries to represent a rebirth after catastrophe...

At one time I felt wounded beyond recovery. I thought that my life was over. Consumed by my suicidal pain, I saw no way out. Some people gave up on me, but others refused to give up hope. Slowly, I was able to rebuild myself after the meltdown, reconstructing a life out of the ashes of my suicidal crisis. Now I try to make my future better and brighter, one day at a time.

A Worse Than Average Day

The day I was going to write this chapter ended up being bad. I wanted to forget about it and make this chapter as positive and hopeful as possible, so I put off writing it until a few days later. Then, I realized that I needed to tell you about that bad day, and how I got through it. Back in the preface to this book, I said that I wanted to show realistic hope, and to be the one who says, "It's dark out there, but I'm going to stay with you till we see daylight." I can't honestly say that I've had some happily-ever-after ending. You probably wouldn't believe me if I did. So, I offer the following example as a way of showing you that it is possible to maintain realistic hope and get through a miserable day with a healthy outlook.

... it is possible to maintain realistic hope and get through a miserable day with a healthy outlook.

For whatever reason, I woke up with a sinking feeling in the pit of my stomach. You might know the type of sensation I'm talking about. It's the plaguing thought that *it's going to be a bad day,* or *damn, I should have stayed in bed.* So, I closed my eyes and told myself, *I can do this, no matter what comes.*

It was time for me to take my car in for an oil change, and as I grabbed my keys to head out of the door, the sensation hit me again. *They're going to find something wrong with the car, and it's going to be expensive to fix.* I dismissed the thought, and re-membered to go back inside for a coupon to cut the cost of the oil change. An hour later, my car was done, and the mechanic said, "By the way, we noticed that your front struts are leaking. We can replace them and do the rear struts at the same time for $600." All I could manage was a deep sigh. *I knew it.*

When I bought the car, I had gotten an extended warranty to avoid large expenses, so I thought the repair just might be covered. Again, there was a nagging thought: *Of course, this is not going to be covered.* I decided to call the warranty company anyhow. I got home, put on my bluetooth phone headset, and tried to turn it on. It wouldn't turn on. *You have got to be kidding me!* I thought. When I called tech support for the headset, they told me I'd have to mail it in to be repaired or replaced. Hanging up the phone, I felt utterly defeated. It was turning out to be a bad day after all. I told myself to take a moment and breathe deeply. *I can still handle this.* When I called the auto warranty company they told me that the car repair would not be covered. I reminded myself that not all days were like this. There were better days. In fact, I played Citizen King's "Better Days" on my computer. It's a rather upbeat song describing a rather pitiful situation. I called my wife, who took a little time out of work to listen empathetically to my litany of mishaps and to encourage me to find something fun to do.

I decided to drive to the post office to send the headset back to the company right away. As I neared the end of my street, a disturbing, suicidal thought entered my mind, but it didn't last long. It would have taken a long time to shake that suicidal feeling in the past. This time, countering the thought was simple: *I can't do that.* I do pay attention to what's *behind* the thought, however. I was feeling frustrated, trapped, and helpless. I hate feeling helpless, so I had to find something that I could definitely accomplish to restore my sense of control.

When I got back home, I picked out the most calming music I know, grabbed an old boombox, and went down to the basement to work on a home improvement project. I started to relax and lose myself in staining the wood for a bigger project (resurfacing the main stairway). Just when I was thinking that the day was turning around, I reached a little too far and accidentally knocked over the container of stain. It was a mess, but it wasn't a disaster, and it was easy enough to clean up. After the situation was under control, I closed my eyes and did some deep breathing while listening to the calming music. At that point, the day seemed so bad that it was almost ridiculous.

I wanted to cry, but all I could do was laugh about what had happened during the day. I told myself: *It's been one of those days, but I've been through this before.* I finished staining the wood, went upstairs and watched *The Empire Strikes Back.* I smiled. *The day is almost over, and tomorrow will probably be better.*

No, it hadn't been a good day. Yet, by the end of it I had gotten my oil changed, learned more about what was covered under my car's warranty, returned a defective product, completed a home improvement project, and watched an enjoyable movie. How did I get through it? Deep breathing, problem solving, music, social support, listening to my emotions, laughter, distraction, and self-reassurance (the thought *I've been through this before*). I also had a therapy appointment scheduled for the next day, so guess what we talked about?

How did I get through it? Deep breathing, problem solving, music, social support, listening to my emotions, laughter, distraction, and self-reassurance (the thought I've been through this before).

Sometimes I have to approach life by getting through the day, and other times I have to tackle one moment at a time. Taking one thing at a time has gotten me through bad moments, bad days, bad weeks, and bad months. You can get through the rough times, too.

The Big Picture

In 1995, I thought my life was over, and I told my friends that I couldn't picture living to see my 19th birthday. Ten years later, I graduated with a Ph.D. from UCLA, married my college sweetheart, and moved to Rochester, New York, to participate in a postdoctoral fellowship program doing what I was most interested in—suicide prevention.

In the intervening years (1996–2005), I founded the first student-led suicide prevention group, watched it collapse, and then watched it be reborn as a chapter of Active Minds on Campus. I struggled financially as a temporary office worker, wondering if I could pay the rent or afford food. Later, I got a grant award from the National Institute of Mental Health to do my research, and now I spend time each week learning a little more about taking care of my finances. There were times when I did public service announcements that encouraged other young people to seek help, and times when I couldn't get health care for myself because I had no insurance. The point is that you never know what's going to happen in the future. Life has its ups and downs, but *it is possible* to get through it all and keep moving forward.

The writing of this book was completed exactly 12 years after my first major suicidal crisis. Once in a while, I still feel depressed, but I work my way through it. Once in a while, I feel a bit manic, but I don't get out of control. Once in a while, suicide comes to mind and beckons me toward death, but such thoughts are fleeting. Most of the time, I am busy working on improving myself, improving my relationships, improving my house, or building my career. I am inspired to keep pushing on by my vision of a hopeful future with a happy family of my own.

What kind of a future would you look forward to? What experiences, accomplishments, or relationships would make it worth your

What experiences, accomplishments, or relationships would make it worth your while to keep living—to find a way to deal with your pain that doesn't involve dying? Those are the images that you need to keep in mind to inspire you to keep living.

while to keep living—to find a way to deal with your pain that doesn't involve dying? Those are the images that you need to keep in mind to inspire you to keep living.

Rebirth: Starting Over

By *rebirth,* I mean taking a hard look at what we believe, and at what we do. It's not easy to change our behavior, especially when confronted with thoughts, emotions, and memories that seem uncontrollable. Yet I try to tell myself that two things will influence what happens in my future—the past and the present. I can't do anything about the past, it's gone. I *can* do something with what's happening to me right now. Any given moment can be the one that is the start of a new life for you, filled with hope and joy. You can't just wait around for that to happen, though—you have to *make* it happen. I like to think that I've come pretty far since my suicidal crisis, but recovery is a long-term process that I keep working on.

After my suicidal crisis, I spent a long time trying to avoid having major mood swings and trying not to upset anyone. It seemed like I only had a tenuous grip on sanity, so I lived cautiously. I was so afraid of losing control that I squelched most emotions altogether. There was a steep price to pay; I lost my passion. Additionally, my life had changed so much that I couldn't go back to being just like I was before. Later, I had to discover what I really valued. Looking into the mirror, I'd ask the guy staring back at me, "What do you believe in? What are you interested in?" I only saw fear in his deep brown eyes, anxiety about not knowing the answers. I had spent so much time as the "guy with bipolar disorder" or "the suicide attempter" that I forgot about other aspects of my identity. I had to figure out who I was, independent of the bipolar disorder and suicide attempts. I started by writing about myself, because my thoughts seem to flow more freely when I'm writing. Maybe for you the thoughts or feelings are easier to capture in music, or art, or dance, or while exercising. The first step to creating a better future is knowing what you want out of life.

As important as it was to figure out who I was, it was also important to realize who I was not. I had to accept that I was not going to be the person with lots of friends who goes to large social gatherings. I usually don't feel comfortable in crowds, and that's okay. There was no need to try to change that part of my personality in order to fit in or to be happy with my life. In the process of rebuilding our lives, we need to separate the parts of us that are authentic from the parts that are based on other people's ideas for how we *should* be.

> In the process of rebuilding our lives, we need to separate the parts of us that are authentic from the parts that are based on other people's ideas for how we should be.

Finally, given my tendency to have strong emotional reactions to certain types of stress, I had to find ways to stay more balanced. In part, that meant taking better care of myself—beginning with learning to let go of the stereotypical male tendency to reject help and "suck it up." I started seeing a psychiatrist, taking my meds on a regular basis, and working with a therapist whenever possible. As I said earlier, our body systems are integrally connected, so I also had to take better care of my health. I started going to my primary care doctor more regularly, trying to get enough sleep each night, improving my nutrition, and increasing my exercise. This combination of taking care of my physical *and* mental health has helped me be a more stable person. With a stable foundation, I can build a life worth living.

Rekindling Happiness From the Ashes

In the last section, I said I can't do anything about the past, it's gone. But obviously the past is still with us, influencing what we do now and in the future. Does that mean the influence is always negative? No. You can draw on the positive or happy experiences from your past to make life better. Over the years, I have tried to go back to some aspects of my past that were associated with positive feelings or memories. In particular, I have sometimes gone back to three past activities that double as distractions, ways to take a break from the stress of the day: playing games, playing music, and watching movies. I have always enjoyed the challenge and instant feedback of video games, so I started playing real-time strategy games. Games also appealed to my appreciation of computer graphics. I revisited some of the old songs and films that I enjoyed while growing up, bringing back good memories. From old school hip hop to 1980s pop songs, I'm able to reconnect to some of the joy that I had when I first heard the songs. I also started collecting DVDs of the movies that I enjoyed in the past. Aside from being able to watch movies like *Back to the Future* or *Rambo III* in the comfort of my home, I can pay less for the films because they are older!

I also enjoyed working on things with my hands in the past, and now that I have recently become a homeowner, that enjoyment is in great demand. I can usually do some kind of repair or improvement project around the house whether I'm feeling okay or feeling depressed. I've found that sometimes it is even *easier* to do some projects when I'm depressed because I approach them more methodically. Even small projects have tangible benefits when I'm done, and it feels good to know that I can still accomplish something. Besides, it takes my mind off of my other problems. Of course, sometimes things go wrong (like spilling some stain), but those are valuable learning experiences that make the next time that much easier. Whether you are doing large projects or simply cleaning up or sorting through a stack of papers, having a sense of accomplishment can brighten up your day.

Finding happiness in the past can be as simple as reconnecting to little things that make you smile. For example, I have always loved dogs, especially beagles. Eventually, I'll get a beagle of my own, but in the meantime I enjoy beagle or puppy calendars, and pictures from The Daily Puppy (http://www.dailypuppy.com). I also love chocolate. Of course, too much chocolate is unhealthy, but in moderation a little chocolate goes a long way toward making me feel better if I'm down.

Honestly, I have struggled with getting back to my art. I used to enjoy drawing immensely. During high school, my friends would tease me for spending so much time drawing—on the school bus, during lunch breaks, in class. After college, I didn't draw as much. I kept telling myself that I just didn't have time to draw, because there was always something else to do. In reality, I have gone back and forth with art, frustrated at not being able to return immediately to the level that I was at before. Eventually, I'm sure that I'll return to my love for art. Who knows? Maybe I'll get back to drawing after this book is published.

Find Your Inner Phoenix

Thank you for reading this book, and I hope it can be one step in your journey to finding hope. The next step is to take some positive action. If you're thinking about ending it all (by suicide), call someone to talk it over first. Talk to a mental health professional. Call the National Suicide Prevention Lifeline at 1-800-273-TALK. *Get all the information you can about the other options you have* and about what your future life might be like.

I feel deeply pained each time I read about someone who died by suicide, or meet someone who attempted suicide or who has seriously considered it. No, I don't know you, or your unique situation, but I have felt the unbearable pain that makes people want to die and I want you to know that there are other ways out of that pain. I am just one of many who have lived through a suicidal crisis and created a better life afterward. My dedication to suicide prevention is based on my unwavering belief that it is possible to make life worthwhile.

I think it is most fitting for me to conclude this book in much the way I started. I do not want you to try (again) to kill yourself. I want you to value *you.* You have the *right* to have a good life. I know that you're worth fighting for.

I want you to value you. You have the right to have a good life. I know that you're worth fighting for.

Frequently Asked Questions

When You Are Recovering From a Suicidal Crisis

What happens if I call a crisis line?

A trained volunteer is likely to pick up the phone and ask about what is happening in your life that is causing the crisis. He or she will listen to you, and ask questions to get more information. If you're looking for resources, he or she will be able to help you find mental health services or other sources of help in your local community.

Can I live a normal life after a suicide attempt?

Short answer: Yes. Longer answer: I'm not really sure what a "normal" life looks like, but you can go on to have a happy and successful life. Everybody has different problems and challenges to overcome throughout life. But by identifying the problems and finding healthy solutions to them, we can overcome those barriers to our goals and dreams. Don't worry, you don't have to do all of that all at once, or all alone—there are many options for getting help.

Whom should I share my suicidal history with?

Sharing any aspect of your past is always a personal decision, particularly when it is something as deeply private and emotional as a suicidal crisis. No matter what you start to tell someone, you can *always* stop talking about it or choose not to reveal particular details. Don't let anyone pressure you into revealing more than you're comfortable with. I've ended up sharing things in the past and have regretted it later. On the other hand, after developing a trusted friendship, I was able to expand my support network by talking about my past suicidal history. Those new friends, who knew about my strengths and problems, were able to help me through stressful times later.

What happens during a psychiatric evaluation?

Whenever you meet with mental health professionals for the first time, they try to get background information about the issue you're concerned with. This information helps them to decide on the most appropriate treatment options to recommend to you. They will ask about your current situation and any symptoms that you may be experiencing. They'll probably ask you about your family (for instance, if anybody you're related to had mental health problems or a history of suicidal behavior) and about your current living situation. They'll also ask you about your drinking, smoking, or drug habits. There will be various other questions, depending on your reason for seeking help, but those are the basics.

Keep two things in mind: (1) Treatment and therapy sessions are confidential; and (2) treatment options depend on your answers in the evaluation. I mention these two things as a way of encouraging you to be honest and open during the evaluation. You will get better treatment that way.

I'm going to a psychiatric hospital. What do I need to know or have before I go in there?

- What health insurance do you have? Make sure you have any insurance card(s) with you. You or your family should call the insurance provider to find out how much of the hospitalization cost it is going to cover.

- Identify a personal advocate. This person will help you figure out what's going on with the hospitalization process and make sure that you are getting good care. Your advocate could be a family member, a friend, or an official Patient Rights Advocate.

- You should know that you have rights as a patient in the hospital, which by law is required to post them in a visible place. For example, you have the right to get treated in a respectful and considerate way, to find out the name of any health care provider working with you, and to get more information about treatment recommendations.

- Pack some things for the hospital stay: In addition to your insurance card, bring photo identification, contact information for your mental health provider and for anyone who should be notified about emergencies, a list of all the medications you're taking (name, dose, and the last time you took them), a list of any medical conditions (asthma, allergies, diabetes, and so forth), sleep wear, toiletries (toothbrush, toothpaste, brush or comb, antiperspirant or deodorant), glasses or contacts, underwear, socks, a book or two to read or study, and some everyday clothes.

- You'll be assigned to a specific ward or unit in the hospital: pediatric (under 18 years old), adult (at least

18 years old generally), or a specialized unit (same gender, same disorder or problem, etc.). Each of these units has its own rules and restrictions that you'll have to adhere to.

What should I consider in choosing a mental health provider?

- The first question to consider is: What do you want to get out of treatment? When you meet a new mental health provider, his or her first question will be something like, "So, what brings you in today?" You can get more out of treatment and figure out if a particular treatment will work for you if you know what your goals are.
- Next, make sure that any mental health professional you are considering is licensed.
- Now, if you are looking for someone to help with a specific issue (like depression or relationships), you might consider trying to find a specialist in that area. More generally, find out if the mental health professional has experience working with adolescents or young adults.
- Finally, consider some practical factors that could affect your treatment. How soon can the provider see you? Do you have transportation to your provider? What insurance does your mental health provider take—how are you going to pay for treatment?
- Once you start working with someone, keep evaluating whether or not you think the treatment is going to help you achieve your goals. If it doesn't seem to be working, talk to your mental health provider about it; together, you'll be able to figure out what to do next.

*I'm worried about going (back) to college. Will I be
able to get through it?*

Short answer: Yes.

Okay, now prepare yourself. I'm going to give you the bad
news first: College can be really stressful. There are so many
new things to adjust to: classes, social life, money issues,
changing relationships with family. It can seem rather overwhelming at times. Now for the good news: College can be a
lot of fun. There are so many new opportunities: classes, social
life, extracurriculars.

How do you handle the potential stress of college? The same
way you would handle the potential stress in life if you weren't
in college. You set long-term goals like graduating, and then
more specific short-term goals. You do your best to take care of
yourself, including working with a mental health provider if
things get overwhelming. You figure out ways to overcome the
barriers that stand in the way of your goals and dreams. Then
you have some fun, enjoy yourself, relax sometimes, and discover even more opportunities for your future. After all, that's
what it means to have good mental *health*.

When Your Family Member or Friend Is in,
or Recovering From, a Suicidal Crisis

*I don't think they're really going to do it. Don't a lot
of people talk about suicide to get attention or to get
others to do something for them?*

Anybody who talks about suicide should be taken seriously
(other significant warning signs that someone may be suicidal
are discussed at length in Chapter 3). It's best not to take a
gamble on whether or not someone will attempt suicide

because the price for being wrong could be death. Some people who talk about suicide do want more attention or some other change in their life. However, if they have become so desperate for attention that they are talking about killing themselves, then there are probably deeper problems that need to be addressed. Take it seriously and get your family member or friend to see a mental health professional. If you're wrong, and the person is just being dramatic, I'm sure he or she will quickly tell you so.

What can I do to help my family member or friend get through a crisis?

- First ask, "Are you thinking about suicide?" or "Are you thinking about killing yourself?" Note: Asking something like "You're not thinking about killing yourself, right?" gives someone the idea that you don't really want to know the truth.

- Okay, so now you've found out that your family member or friend is in the middle of a suicidal crisis. Now what? Stay as calm as possible. Remember that there are many options available that could be helpful (for you, too).

- Listen. Let her or him tell you about the stress and the emotional pain that are behind the suicidal feelings. It is always hard to listen to someone talk about immense pain without your reacting right away—either by being judgmental or by offering advice. Believe me, though, you are already helping by listening with empathy.

- Next, ensure your family member or friend's safety by (1) helping him or her get rid of anything dangerous that could be used in a suicide attempt (guns, pills, etc.); and (2) staying with him or her until you can get some help.

- Once short-term safety is under control, persuade your family member or friend to talk to a mental health provider. Offer to go with him or her for help. If nobody is available at the time and you are worried, call the National Suicide Prevention Lifeline (1-800-273-TALK) and talk to someone who can help you or help the other person directly.

- Ask the person you are concerned about who else could be included in the discussions about how to get help—like other family members, friends, and any mental health providers that the person may already have been seeing.

What can I do to support my family member or friend in the long term?

As in the crisis situation, one of the most helpful things you can do is to let the person know that you are available for him or her to talk to—that you are willing to listen. Do what you would do ordinarily to be a good parent, sibling, or friend. If the person is close by, then visit and plan activities together. If the person is far away, call, text, or e-mail him or her. If the person is talking about suicide, remind him or her about all the other options available.

I could offer other advice, but this next one is *the most important advice* I can give about how to be supportive: Ask your family member or friend what would be helpful. If he or she can't think of anything, then find out what was helpful in the past and try that. The only caveat is to also trust your instincts. For example, if your family member or friend says something like "It would help if you leave me alone," that's probably not really going to help. You could respond with, "Okay, that's one option, what other options do we have?" or "When should I come back to talk about what I can do to help?" Eventually, you'll find out what unique blend of supports the person values the most.

General Questions

Is it possible to prevent suicide?

Yes, generally it is possible to prevent suicide. Our chances of successfully preventing suicide improve greatly when we can intervene and help someone early on, before the suicidal crisis ever develops.

Does asking about suicide make people think about suicide?

No. If you're worried about someone being suicidal, then suicide has probably already crossed his or her mind. The most time-tested way to find out just what the person really thinks about suicide is to ask. You might be scared that your friend will actually say yes. That's normal. Death and suicide are scary topics. After years in suicide prevention, I'm still terrified of a yes response to those questions, *but I still ask.* Trust me, the chance of suicide is greater if you don't speak up about your feelings. Research shows that suicide isn't caused just by talking about it. The person may even be relieved because he or she has someone to talk to.

If someone tells me about suicidal feelings, but asks me to keep them a secret, should I honor that request and keep it to myself?

No. I know you want to honor the request for secrecy, most likely because you value the person who asked you to keep the secret. However, you demonstrate that you value the person and the person's *life* by summoning help. I was incredibly angry with my friends when they shared my suicidal feelings with others. I may have even said that I would never forgive them. But I didn't stay mad for more than a couple of months, and in the end, they played a vital role in preventing my suicide. I'm sure you'll agree that alive and angry is better than dead and silent.

Is Christmastime when most suicides happen?

Actually, it is almost the opposite. Slightly more suicides occur in the spring and summer than in the winter months. However, some people do get very depressed around Christmastime. Generally, the depression is due to loneliness, missing family or friends, or the winter weather. Some people are consistently affected by changes in the weather, with darker winter days bringing depression and bright summer days bringing upswings. When the mood changes are dramatic and interfere with life, they may be due to seasonal affective disorder, and treatments are available to help with this condition.

Are people who attempt suicide different from people who die by suicide?

I wish I could give you a simple answer, but it's a complex question. Some people injure themselves (using methods such as cutting or burning) without wanting to die, whereas others injure themselves with at least some intent to die. For the "suicidal" group, the people who do have some intent to die, most will live through the injury (suicide attempt) while some will die (suicide). The majority of people who have attempted suicide do not kill themselves in the future, although researchers do know that people who die by suicide are very likely to have attempted it in the past, so one or more suicide attempts does increase the risk of suicide in the future.

The bottom line: If someone is thinking about injuring himself or herself (or already has done so), the issue of intent is less relevant than the extent to which that person is suffering from severe emotional pain. That person needs *help* now, and we should do whatever we can, as a family member or friend, to persuade that person to get help from a mental health professional immediately.

Does everyone think about suicide at some time?

Probably. Most people dismiss the idea fairly quickly. This is the main reason why the topic of suicide finds its way casually into television shows, movies, music, jokes, and everyday conversation. It becomes a dangerous idea, though, when someone spends a lot of time thinking about suicide or starts making plans for suicide.

What is the main cause of suicide?

The vast majority of people who die by suicide have a mental health problem, such as depression, and either they are not getting any help for the problem or the help they are getting isn't adequate.

What is the most frequent method of suicide?

In general, most suicide deaths are caused by guns. However, most recently, for adolescent girls, suffocation is the leading method of suicide.

Do most people who die by suicide leave a suicide note?

No. Although some people (12%–37%) leave a suicide note, most do not. Because suicide notes give some information about a person's final thoughts, those cases tend to get more attention in the media and in some types of research.

Glossary

addiction A mental disorder characterized by the recurring compulsion to engage in some specific activity, such as drug or alcohol consumption, accompanied by tolerance and withdrawal symptoms if that activity ceases suddenly.

advocacy group An organization that works on changing a social issue, such as reducing the number of suicides.

advocate A person who works on changing a social issue or advancing a cause.

altruism Giving to other people, or doing things for others, without expecting anything in return.

amygdala The part of the brain that is responsible for emotional memories.

anticonvulsant A medication that helps prevent seizures. Many anticonvulsants have mood-stabilizing effects as well.

antidepressant A medication used to prevent or relieve depression.

antipsychotic A term describing a varied group of drugs used to treat severe mental disorders involving psychotic symptoms.

anxiety disorder Any of several mental disorders that are characterized by extreme or maladaptive feelings of tension, fear, or worry.

benzodiazepine A psychoactive drug that acts as a mild tranquilizer.

bipolar disorder A disorder characterized by an overly high mood, called mania, which alternates with depression.

cognitive-behavioral therapy (CBT) A form of psychotherapy that aims to change habitual patterns of thinking and behavior that may be contributing to a person's problems.

comorbidity The presence of two or more disorders, such as depression and substance abuse, in the same person.

conduct disorder A disorder characterized by a repetitive or persistent pattern of having extreme difficulty following rules or conforming to social norms.

constriction   When someone's mind narrows onto a specific topic, such as suicide, to the exclusion of everything else.

contagion   When one person's suicidal behavior influences other people who are vulnerable to suicidal feelings to act on their suicidal urges as well.

cortisol   A hormone released by the adrenal glands that is responsible for many of the physiological effects of stress.

counseling   A process in which one talks to a mental health professional to identify and address issues, concerns, problems, or stress. Often used interchangeably with the term *therapy*.

culturally appropriate   Attitudes, values, and practices that are effective in working with a variety of cultures. This may include honoring and respecting the language, beliefs, and customs of people who are getting mental health services.

day treatment   See partial hospitalization.

delusion   An irrational belief that cannot be altered with rational argument.

depression   A disorder that involves being in a low mood nearly all the time or losing interest or enjoyment in almost everything. These feelings last for at least two weeks and cause significant distress or problems in everyday life.

detoxification   The process of medically removing a chemical from one's body.

diagnosis   A medical name or label for a pattern of symptoms or problems.

dialectical-behavioral therapy (DBT)   A form of psychotherapy that aims to help one control suicidal impulses through learning to cope with one's negative emotions and emotional situations.

distraction   A coping strategy that enables one to do an engaging activity that can take his or her mind off a stressful problem.

dopamine   A neurotransmitter that is involved in depression, pleasurable feelings, and movement.

dual diagnosis   A situation in which one person is diagnosed with both a mental illness and chemical dependency.

eating disorder   A disorder characterized by serious disturbances in eating behavior. People may severely restrict what they eat, or they may go on eating binges, then try to compensate by means such as self-induced vomiting or misuse of laxatives.

effective   Programs or activities that have been evaluated in scientific studies and shown to decrease problems or to increase health.

electroconvulsive therapy (ECT)   A treatment for depression that involves delivering a carefully controlled electrical current to the brain, where it produces a brief seizure. This is thought to alter some of the electrical and chemical processes involved in brain functioning.

emotional dysregulation   Emotional reactions to negative events that are more intense, more frequent, or more long-lasting than they are for the average person.

emotionality   A long-term pattern of emotional dysregulation that has become a personality trait.

emotional pain   See psychological pain.

endorphins   Chemicals found within the brain that are associated with feelings of well-being.

euphoria   A state of very intense happiness and feelings of well-being.

family therapy   A form of psychotherapy in which several members of a family participate in therapy sessions together under the guidance of a therapist.

gamma-amino-butyric acid (GABA)   A neurotransmitter that inhibits the flow of nerve signals in neurons by blocking the release of other neurotransmitters. It is thought to help quell anxiety.

generic medication   A medication that is the same chemical compound as a named prescription drug, but produced by another (usually less expensive) company.

genetics   The scientific study of how traits or characteristics are biologically passed from one generation to the next.

group therapy   A form of psychotherapy in which a group of people with similar problems work on specific issues together under the guidance of a therapist.

hallucination   A false perception of something that is not really there; hallucinations may be visual (sight), auditory (hearing), tactile (touch), gustatory (taste), or olfactory (smell) perceptions.

health   Complete health, involving physical and mental wellness.

health care   Professional services that are designed to improve one's health.

health care professional   A person who has received specific training to provide health care services. Also called a health care provider.

health insurance   A type of contract that pays for certain health care costs incurred when a person gets sick or injured.

health maintenance organization (HMO)   A health insurance organization that provides care through a specific list of health care providers.

hospitalization   Inpatient treatment in a facility that provides intensive, specialized care and close, round-the-clock monitoring.

hypothalamic-pituitary-adrenal (HPA) axis   A pathway of communication within the body that goes from the hypothalamus to the pituitary gland in the brain down to the adrenal glands near the kidneys. The primary function of this pathway is gearing up the body to respond to stress or threats.

impulsivity   Taking immediate action based on an urge or strong feeling, usually without thinking through the consequences of the action beforehand.

insomnia   Trouble falling or staying asleep, or getting sleep of such poor quality that the person doesn't feel rested and refreshed the next morning.

interpersonal therapy (IPT)   A form of psychotherapy that aims to address the interpersonal triggers for mental, emotional, or behavioral symptoms.

lethal means   Items or materials that could be used in a potentially deadly suicide plan.

lithium   A mood-stabilizing medication.

major depression   A disorder that involves being either depressed or irritable nearly all the time, or losing interest or enjoyment in almost everything. These feelings last for at least two weeks. They are associated with several other symptoms, and they cause significant distress or difficulty with everyday activities.

mania   An overly high mood that lasts for at least a week or leads to dangerous behavior. Symptoms include overblown ideas, racing thoughts, risk taking, extreme irritability, decreased need for sleep, and increased talkativeness or activity.

manic depression   See bipolar disorder.

Medicaid   A government program that provides medical and mental health care to eligible low-income and disabled individuals.

medication   Chemicals formulated to have specific actions that decrease symptoms of illness or improve health; most are prescribed to be taken by mouth, but others are injected or inhaled.

mental disorder   An illness characterized by abnormalities in the way that a person thinks, feels, or acts. To be called a disorder, these abnormalities must cause the person distress or interfere with the person's ability to function.

mental health   A state of mental and emotional wellness that could include positive emotions, hopefulness, and a sense that life is worth living.

mental health problem   An issue that interferes with a person's mental health, but not to the point where it would qualify as a mental disorder.

mental health professional   A person who has received specific training to provide services that address mental health problems or disorders and that improve mental health. Also called a mental health provider.

mental health services   Professional services that are specifically designed to address mental health problems or disorders and to improve mental health.

mental illness   See mental disorder.

mixed state   A bipolar episode that is characterized by a mixture of mania and depression occurring at the same time.

monoamine oxidase inhibitor (MAOI)   An older class of antidepressant that is rarely prescribed for young people.

mood   A pervasive emotion that colors a person's whole view of the world.

mood disorder   A mental disorder in which a disturbance of mood is the chief feature.

mood stabilizer   A medication for bipolar disorder that reduces manic and/or depressive symptoms and helps even out mood swings.

negative life events   Stressful or harmful life experiences that can increase the risk for mental health problems or suicidal behavior.

neuron   A nerve cell that is specially designed to send information to other nerve, muscle, or gland cells.

neuroticism   See emotionality.

neurotransmitter   A natural chemical that brain cells use to communicate with each other.

norepinephrine   A neurotransmitter that may be involved in depression, suicidal behavior, and other mental health problems.

omega-3 fatty acids   Natural substances found in fish oil that are also sold as dietary supplements.

opiate   A narcotic chemical found in opium.

opioid   A chemical substance that has an opiate-like effect in the brain.

outpatient treatment   A treatment option where you live at home and go to school as usual, but occasionally see a doctor or therapist.

panic attack   A sudden, unexpected wave of intense fear and apprehension that is accompanied by physical symptoms, such as a racing or pounding heart, shortness of breath, and sweating.

panic disorder   An anxiety disorder characterized by the repeated occurrence and fear of spontaneous panic attacks. The fear results from the belief that such attacks will result in catastrophes, such as having a heart attack.

paranoia   A disturbed thought process characterized by unreasonable anxiety, fear, and/or delusions of persecution.

partial hospitalization   A treatment option where you spend at least four hours a day on therapy and other treatment-related services, but go home at night.

patient assistance program   A special program that many pharmaceutical (drug) companies have implemented to provide medication to people who do not have insurance or money to pay for health care.

physical therapy   A health profession that uses exercises, massage, hot or cold treatments, and other techniques to help people regain body function after sustaining an injury or disability.

placebo   A sugar pill that looks like a real medication but doesn't contain any active ingredient.

positive psychology   A field of psychology that is primarily concerned with factors that promote growth, healthy development, positive experiences, and well-being.

positive youth development   Developmental studies, or application of developmental studies, that focus on the positive psychology of youth and young adults.

preferred provider organization (PPO)   A health insurance organization that provides care through most health care providers, but pays more of the expenses for professionals on a specific list.

prescription drugs / prescription medication   See medication.

prevention   An approach to health concerns that seeks to stop problems before they fully develop.

protective factor   A situation, event, or circumstance that decreases a person's chances of developing a disorder or problem.

psychiatric disorder   See mental disorder.

psychiatric hospital   A type of hospital that provides mental health services with at least one overnight stay for people who need intensive care.

psychiatric ilness   See mental disorder.

psychiatrist   A medical doctor who specializes in the diagnosis and treatment of mental illnesses and emotional problems.

psychiatry   The medical practice that addresses the development, identification, and treatment of mental disorders.

psychodynamic therapy   A form of psychotherapy that aims to help people work out the interactions between their past issues and their current problems (dynamics).

psychological pain   Intense, overwhelming, and intolerable negative emotions, such as sadness, depression, anxiety, anger, guilt, loneliness, or shame.

psychologist   A mental health professional who provides assessment and treatment for mental and emotional disorders.

psychology   The scientific study of human behavior, including factors related to mental health problems and mental disorders.

psychosis   A symptom of severe mental illness characterized by delusions, hallucinations, and/or disordered thinking.

psychotherapy   The treatment of a mental disorder with "talk therapy" and other psychological techniques. Also called therapy or counseling.

quality of life   A person's subjective sense of satisfaction with life.

receptor   A molecule that recognizes a specific chemical, such as a neurotransmitter. For a chemical message to be sent from one nerve cell to another, the message must be delivered to a matching receptor on the surface of the receiving nerve cell.

recovery   The process of regaining health and hope after illness or injury.

reuptake   The process by which a neurotransmitter is absorbed back into the sending branch of the nerve cell that originally released it.

reward circuit   A group of sections and structures in the brain that work together to produce feelings of pleasure and satisfaction in response to certain stimuli.

risk factor   A situation, event, or circumstance that increases a person's chances of developing a disorder or problem.

S-adenosyl-L-methionine (SAM-e)   A natural compound that is sold as a dietary supplement.

schizophrenia   A severe mental disorder that produces symptoms such as distorted thoughts and perceptions, disorganized speech and behavior, and a reduced ability to feel emotions.

seasonal affective disorder (SAD)   A form of depression in which the symptoms come and go around the same time each year. Typically, the symptoms begin in the fall or winter and subside in the spring or summer.

selective serotonin reuptake inhibitor (SSRI)   A type of antidepressant medication that stops serotonin from being recycled by brain cells, thus increasing the amount of serotonin available for brain functions.

self-concept   A person's complete subjective impression of himself or herself, including strengths, weaknesses, and future possibilities.

self-efficacy   A person's beliefs about what he or she can accomplish; the perception of one's abilities.

self-esteem   Respect or positive feelings about oneself.

serotonin   A neurotransmitter that is involved in depression, aggression, impulsivity, suicidal behavior, sleep, and other functions.

side effects   Unintended consequences of treatments, particularly medications.

sliding scale   An approach to payment for services that is based on one's income or ability to pay for those services.

social support   The support and assistance one receives from other people, which can range from emotional support (e.g., listening to one's problems) to providing financial assistance.

social work   The profession that focuses on addressing the social conditions of a person or community. Someone who practices social work (the social worker) may help a person through counseling or assistance with finding a home or job.

St. John's wort   (*Hypericum perforatum*) An herb that is a popular dietary supplement.

State Child Health Insurance Program (SCHIP)   A government program that provides free or low-cost insurance coverage for children and teenagers whose families meet eligibility criteria.

stigma   Shame or rejection that is attached to a particular label or characteristic of a group of people.

stressor   An event or circumstance that causes stress.

stress response   The body's response to any perceived threat, whether real or imagined, physical or psychological. It sets off physiological changes, such as an increase in heart rate, blood pressure, breathing rate, and muscle tension.

substance abuse   A person's consumption of alcohol or drugs that has gotten "out of control," resulting in social, financial, or legal problems. When the use of alcohol, prescription medications, or street drugs begins to interfere with a person's life, then it is crossing the line into substance abuse.

suicidal behavior   Actions that a person takes with the intent of killing himself or herself, including suicide attempts and suicide. Usually these actions consist of some type of injury, poisoning, or suffocation that the person inflicts on himself or herself.

suicidal crisis   The period when someone is frequently experiencing suicidal ideation and may engage in suicidal behavior.

suicidal ideation   Thoughts about engaging in suicidal behavior.

suicide   Suicidal behavior that results in death.

suicide attempt   Suicidal behavior that does not cause death and may not leave evidence of injury.

suicide survivors   The people who knew someone who died by suicide. Usually the term is applied to family members and significant others.

support group   A group that brings together people with a common concern so they can share support, encouragement, and hands-on advice.

symptoms   Signs that indicate that someone may have a particular illness, disorder, or condition.

therapy   See counseling; psychotherapy.

tolerance   The effect whereby a person's reaction to a drug decreases so that higher and higher doses are required to produce the desired effect.

tricyclic antidepressant   An older type of depression medication.

well-being   A positive experience of life, generally including happiness and good health.

withdrawal   A set of symptoms that appear when a person abruptly ceases use of a substance upon which he or she has become dependent.

Resources

Crisis Hotline

National Suicide Prevention Lifeline
(800) 273-TALK (8255)
www.suicidepreventionlifeline.org
Connect to a local crisis center 24/7.

Organizations

Active Minds on Campus
1875 Connecticut Ave., NW, Suite 418
Washington, DC 20009
www.activemindsoncampus.org
National organization that focuses on college mental health, with affiliated groups
on college and university campuses throughout the United States.

American Academy of Child and Adolescent Psychiatry
3615 Wisconsin Ave., NW
Washington, DC 20016-3007
(202) 966-7300
www.aacap.org
Professional association for psychiatrists specializing in children and adolescents.
Psychiatrist directory: www.aacap.org/ReferralDirectory/index.htm

American Association of Suicidology
5221 Wisconsin Ave., NW
Washington, DC 20015
(202) 237-2280
www.suicidology.org
Professional organization that focuses on understanding, training, and preventing suicide.

American Foundation for Suicide Prevention
120 Wall St., 22nd Floor
New York, NY 10005
(888) 333-2377
(212) 363-3500
www.afsp.org
Private foundation that funds suicide prevention research and support groups for suicide survivors.

American Psychiatric Association
1000 Wilson Blvd., Suite 1825
Arlington, VA 22209
(888) 357-7924
www.psych.org
Professional association for psychiatrists.

American Psychological Association
750 First St., NE
Washington, DC 20002
(800) 374-2721
www.apa.org
Professional association for psychologists.
Information and psychologist directory: www.apahelpcenter.org

Centre for Suicide Prevention
1202 Centre St., SE, Suite 320
Calgary, AB T2G 5A5
Canada
(403) 245-3900
Canadian organization for suicide prevention that has general information and resources specifically for Canadians.

International Association for Suicide Prevention
I.A.S.P. Central Administrative Office
Le Barade
F-32330 Gondrin
France
+33 562 29 19 47
www.med.uio.no/iasp/
Source for international contacts and information on suicide prevention.

The Jed Foundation
583 Broadway, Suite 8B
New York, NY 10012
(212) 647-7544
www.jedfoundation.org
Organization focused on college suicide prevention and mental health.
Online mental health resource, with specific information for many colleges: www.
    ulifeline.org

Mental Health America (formerly National Mental Health Association)
2001 N. Beauregard St., 12th Floor
Alexandria, VA 22311
(703) 684-7722
www.nmha.org
Organization that seeks to help "ALL people live mentally healthier lives," with state
    and community affiliates.

Mental Health Infosource
www.mhsource.com
General information about mental health, including e-mail newsletters on a variety
    of mental health problems.

National Alliance on Mental Illness (NAMI)
Colonial Place Three
2107 Wilson Blvd., Suite 300
Arlington, VA 22201-3042
(703) 524-7600
www.nami.org
Supports people with mental illness and their families with state and community
    affiliates. NAMI also has free information about psychiatric disorders, medi-
    cations, and other related topics.

National Association of Social Workers
750 First St., NE, Suite 700
Washington, DC 20002
(202) 408-8600
www.socialworkers.org
Professional association of social workers.
Information and directory of social workers: www.helpstartshere.org

National Institute of Mental Health
Office of Communications
6001 Executive Blvd.
Rm. 8184, MSC 9663
Bethesda, MD 20892-9663
(866) 615-6464
www.nimh.nih.gov
Division of the National Institutes of Health (U.S. government health research) that
focuses on research about mental illness and mental health issues.

National Mental Health Consumer's Self-Help Clearinghouse
1211 Chestnut St., Suite 1207
Philadelphia, PA 19107
(800) 553-4539
(215) 751-1810
www.mhselfhelp.org
Information about various ways for people with mental health problems to help
themselves or help each other.

National Organization for People of Color Against Suicide
P.O. Box 75571
Washington, DC 20013
(202) 549-6039
www.nopcas.org
Organization that focuses on suicide prevention among racial and ethnic minority
groups.

Substance Abuse and Mental Health Services Administration
National Mental Health Information Center
P.O. Box 42557
Washington, DC 20015
(800) 789-2647
www.mentalhealth.samhsa.gov
Gateway to many U.S. government mental health services and programs.

Suicide Awareness Voices of Education
8120 Penn Avenue South, Suite 470
Bloomington, MN 55431
(952) 946-7998
www.save.org
Organization focused on a national public awareness campaign, education
and training, and resource distribution for suicide prevention and grief after
suicide.

Suicide Prevention Action Network USA
1025 Vermont Ave., NW, Suite 1066
Washington, DC 20005
(202) 449-3600
www.spanusa.org
Organization dedicated to suicide prevention through education, awareness, and
community action. Web site has easy ways to keep up with U.S. government
action related to suicide prevention or mental health, and to contact government
representatives to voice support.

Suicide Prevention Resource Center
Education Development Center, Inc.
55 Chapel St.
Newton, MA 02458-1060
877-GET-SPRC (877-438-7772)
www.sprc.org
Source of information and training. Customized information is available depending
on your role (teen, college student, teacher, etc.), along with an online library.

The Trevor Project
Administrative Offices
9056 Santa Monica Blvd., Ste. 100
West Hollywood, CA 90069
www.thetrevorproject.org
Organization that focuses on suicide prevention among gay and lesbian youth.

Volunteers in Healthcare
111 Brewster St.
Pawtucket, RI 02860
(401) 729-3284
www.rxassist.org
Organization affiliated with Brown University that provides information and application help for Patient Assistance Programs where low-income individuals or
families can get free (or low-cost) medications.

Books

Suicidal Crisis: First-Person Accounts

Blauner, Susan R. *How I Stayed Alive When My Brain Was Trying to Kill Me: One Person's Guide to Suicide Prevention.* New York: William Morrow & Co., hardcover 2002; Quill Paperbacks, 2003.

Chabot, John A. *A New Lease on Life: Facing the World After a Suicide Attempt.* Minneapolis, MN: Fairview, 1997.

Clemons, James T., (Ed.). *Children of Jonah: Personal Stories by Survivors of Suicide Attempts.* Herndon, VA: Capital Books, Inc., 2001.

Heckler, Richard A. *Waking Up Alive: The Descent, the Suicide Attempt, and the Return to Life.* New York: Ballantine, 1994.

Jamison, Kay R. *An Unquiet Mind: A Memoir of Moods and Madness.* New York: Knopf, 1995.

Styron, William. *Darkness Visible: A Memoir of Madness.* New York: Vintage, 1992.

Taylor, Kevin. *Seduction of Suicide: Understanding and Recovering From an Addiction to Suicide.* Bloomington, IN: Authorhouse, 2002.

Wise, Terry L. *Waking Up: Climbing Through the Darkness.* Oxnard, CA: Pathfinder Publishing, 2003.

Suicide and Suicide Prevention: General

Arena, Jillayne. *Step Back from the Exit: 45 Reasons to Say No to Suicide.* Milwaukee, WI: Zebulon Press, 1995.

Clemons, James T. *What Does the Bible Say About Suicide?* (2nd ed.). Minneapolis, MN: Fortress Press, 1990.

Colt, George H. *November of the Soul: The Enigma of Suicide.* New York: Scribner, 2006.

Jamison, Kay R. *Night Falls Fast: Understanding Suicide.* New York: Knopf, 1999.

Nelson, Richard E., and Judith C. Galas. *The Power to Prevent Suicide: A Guide for Teens Helping Teens.* Minneapolis, MN: Free Spirit, 1994.

Quinnett, Paul G. *Suicide—The Forever Decision: For Those Thinking About Suicide, and for Those Who Know, Love, or Counsel Them.* New York: Crossroad Classic, 1987. (Available for download through www.qprinstitute.com.)

Rickgarn, Ralph L.V. *Perspectives on College Student Suicide.* Amityville, NY: Baywood Publishing Company, Inc., 1994.

Shneidman, Edwin S. *The Suicidal Mind.* New York: Oxford University Press, 1998.

Traff, Catherine S. *The Calm Before the Storm: Recognizing When the Decision to Suicide Is Made.* Edmonton, Alberta: Turtle Pond Publishing, 2004.

Related Issues

Bower, Sharon A., and Gordon H. Bower. *Asserting Yourself: A Practical Guide for Positive Change* (updated edition). Reading, MA: Addison-Wesley Publishing Company, 1991.

Burns, David D. *Ten Days to Self-Esteem.* New York: Quill, 1993.

Cobain, Bev. *When Nothing Matters Anymore: A Survival Guide for Depressed Teens.* Minneapolis, MN: Free Spirit, 1998.

Copeland, Mary Ellen, and Stuart Copans. *Recovering from Depression: A Workbook for Teens* (rev. ed.). Baltimore, MD: Paul H. Brookes, 2002.

Web Sites

MindZone, Annenberg Foundation Trust at Sunnylands with the Annenberg Public Policy Center of the University of Pennsylvania, www.CopeCareDeal.org

TeensHealth, Nemours Foundation, www.teenshealth.org

Wellness Recovery Action Plan, www.mentalhealthrecovery.com

Help for Related Problems

Anxiety Disorders

ORGANIZATIONS

Anxiety Disorders Association of America
(240) 485-1001
www.adaa.org

Freedom From Fear
(718) 351-1717
www.freedomfromfear.org

BOOKS

Ford, Emily, with Michael R. Liebowitz, M.D., and Linda Wasmer Andrews. *What You Must Think of Me: A Firsthand Account of One Teenager's Experience With Social Anxiety Disorder.* New York: Oxford University Press with the Annenberg Foundation Trust at Sunnylands and the Annenberg Public Policy Center at the University of Pennsylvania, 2007.

Kant, Jared, with Martin Franklin, Ph.D., and Linda Wasmer Andrews. *The Thought That Counts: A Firsthand Account of One Teenager's Experience with Obsessive-Compulsive Disorder.* New York: Oxford University Press with the Annenberg Foundation Trust at Sunnylands and the Annenberg Public Policy Center at the University of Pennsylvania, 2008.

Eating Disorders

ORGANIZATIONS
National Association of Anorexia Nervosa and Associated Disorders
(847) 831-3438
www.anad.org

National Eating Disorders Association
(206) 382-3587
www.nationaleatingdisorders.org

BOOK
Arnold, Carrie, with B. Timothy Walsh, M.D. *Next to Nothing: A Firsthand Account of One Teenager's Experience With an Eating Disorder.* New York: Oxford University Press with the Annenberg Foundation Trust at Sunnylands and the Annenberg Public Policy Center at the University of Pennsylvania, 2007.

Mood Disorders

ORGANIZATIONS
Child and Adolescent Bipolar Foundation
(847) 256-8525
www.cabf.org

Depression and Bipolar Support Alliance
(800) 826-3632
www.dbsalliance.org

Depression and Related Affective Disorders Association
(410) 583-2919
www.drada.org

Families for Depression Awareness
(781) 890-0220
www.familyaware.org

BOOKS

Irwin, Cait, with Dwight L. Evans, M.D., and Linda Wasmer Andrews. *Monochrome Days: A Firsthand Account of One Teenager's Experience With Depression.* New York: Oxford University Press with the Annenberg Foundation Trust at Sunnylands and the Annenberg Public Policy Center at the University of Pennsylvania, 2007.

Jamieson, Patrick E., Ph.D., with Moira A. Rynn, M.D. *Mind Race: A Firsthand Account of One Teenager's Experience With Bipolar Disorder.* New York: Oxford University Press with the Annenberg Foundation Trust at Sunnylands and the Annenberg Public Policy Center at the University of Pennsylvania, 2006.

Substance Abuse

ORGANIZATIONS

American Council for Drug Education
(800) 488-3784
www.acde.org

National Council on Alcoholism and Drug Dependence
(800) 622-2255
www.ncadd.org

National Institute on Alcohol Abuse and Alcoholism
(301) 443–3860
www.niaaa.nih.gov
www.collegedrinkingprevention.gov

National Institute on Drug Abuse
(301) 443-1124
www.drugabuse.gov
www.teens.drugabuse.gov

Substance Abuse and Mental Health Services Administration
(800) 729-6686
www.samhsa.gov

BOOK

Keegan, Kyle, with Howard B. Moss, M.D. *Chasing the High: A Firsthand Account of One Young Person's Experience With Substance Abuse.* New York: Oxford

University Press with the Annenberg Foundation Trust at Sunnylands and the Annenberg Public Policy Center at the University of Pennsylvania, 2008.

Schizophrenia

ORGANIZATIONS
National Schizophrenia Foundation
(800) 482-9534
www.nsfoundation.org

World Fellowship for Schizophrenia and Allied Disorders
(416) 961-2855
www.world-schizophrenia.org

BOOKS

Schiller, Lori, and Amanda Bennet. *The Quiet Room: A Journey Out of the Torment of Madness.* New York: Grand Central Publishing, 1996.

Snyder, Kurt, with Raquel E. Gur, M.D., Ph.D., and Linda Wasmer Andrews. *Me, Myself, and Them: A Firsthand Account of One Young Person's Experience With Schizophrenia.* New York: Oxford University Press with the Annenberg Foundation Trust at Sunnylands and the Annenberg Public Policy Center at the University of Pennsylvania, 2007.

Wagner, Pamela Spiro, and Carolyn S. Spiro. *Divided Minds: Twin Sisters and Their Journey Through Schizophrenia.* New York: St. Martin's Press, 2005.

Bibliography

American Association of Suicidology. Understanding and Helping the Suicidal Person. Available: http://www.suicidology.org/associations/1045/files/Understanding .pdf. Accessed: September 14, 2007.

American Association of Suicidology. Youth Suicide Fact Sheet (December 28, 2006). Available: http://www.suicidology.org/associations/1045/files/Youth2004 .pdf. Accessed: September 14, 2007.

American College Health Association. American College Health Association—National College Health Assessment (ACHA-NCHA) Web Summary (August 2007). Available at http://www.acha-ncha.org/data_highlights.html. Accessed: September 14, 2007.

American Foundation for Suicide Prevention. About Suicide: Frequently Asked Questions. Available: http://www.afsp.org Accessed: September 14, 2007.

Amin, Zenab, Turhan Canli, and C. Neill Epperson. Effect of estrogen–serotonin interactions on mood and cognition. *Behavioral and Cognitive Neuroscience Review* 4 (2005): 43–58.

Andreason, N.J. and A. Canter. The creative writer: psychiatric symptoms and family history. *Comprehensive Psychiatry* 15 (1974): 123–31.

Baumeister, Roy F. Suicide as escape from self. *Psychological Review* 97 (1990): 90–113.

Birger, Moshe, Marnina Swartz, David Cohen, Ya'akov Alesh, Chaim Grishpan, and Moshe Koteir. Aggression: The testosterone–serotonin link. *The Israeli Medical Association Journal* 5 (2003): 653–658.

Bower, Sharon A., and Gordon H. Bower. *Asserting Yourself: A Practical Guide for Positive Change* (updated ed.). Reading, MA: Addison-Wesley Publishing Company, Inc., 1991.

Brown, Gregory K. Cognitive therapy for suicide prevention: Building hope for the future. Presented at Suicide Prevention Action Network 12th Annual National Suicide Prevention Awareness & Training Event, July 20, 2007.

Brown, Jocelyn, Patricia Cohen, Jeffrey G. Johnson, and Elizabeth M. Smailes. Childhood abuse and neglect: Specificity of effects on adolescent and young adult depression and suicidality. *Journal of the American Academy of Child and Adolescent Psychiatry* 38 (1999): 1490–1496.

Centers for Disease Control and Prevention. Suicide Trends Among Youths and Young Adults Aged 10–24 Years—United States, 1990–2004. *Morbidity and Mortality Weekly Report* 56 (2007): 905–908.

Centers for Disease Control and Prevention. Youth Risk Behavior Surveillance—United States, 2005. Surveillance Summaries, *Morbidity and Mortality Weekly Report* 55 (2006): SS-5.

Centers for Disease Control and Prevention. Youth Risk Behavior Surveillance: National College Health Risk Behavior Survey—United States, 1995. Surveillance Summaries, *Morbidity and Mortality Weekly Report* 46 (1997): SS-6.

Centers for Disease Control and Prevention, National Injury Prevention and Control. *Web-based Injury Statistics Query and Reporting System (WISQARS)*. Available: http://www.cdc.gov/ncipc/wisqars

Centre for Suicide Prevention. Information: F.A.Q.: Questions About Suicide. Available: http://www.suicideinfo.ca/csp/go.aspx?tabid=30. Accessed: September 14, 2007.

Conner, Kenneth R., Paul R. Duberstein, Yeates Conwell, and Eric D. Caine. Reactive aggression and suicide: Theory and evidence. *Aggression and Violent Behavior* 8 (2003): 413–432.

Conner, Kenneth R., Paul R. Duberstein, Yeates Conwell, Larry Seidlitz, and Eric D. Caine. Psychological vulnerability to completed suicide: A review of empirical studies. *Suicide and Life-Threatening Behavior* 31 (2001): 367–385.

Enns, Murray W., Brian J. Cox, and Mohamed Inayatulla. Personality predictors of outcome for adolescents hospitalized for suicidal ideation. *Journal of the American Academy of Child and Adolescent Psychiatry* 42 (2003): 720–727.

Evans, Dwight L., Edna B. Foa, Raquel E. Gur, Herbert Hendin, Charles P. O'Brien, Martin E. P. Seligman, and B. Timothy Walsh (Eds.). *Treating and Preventing Adolescent Mental Health Disorders: What We Know and What We Don't Know*. New York: Oxford University Press with the Annenberg Foundation Trust at Sunnylands and the Annenberg Public Policy Center of the University of Pennsylvania, 2005.

Fink, George, Barbara Sumner, Roberta Rosie, Helen Wilson, and Judith McQueen. Androgen actions on central serotonin neurotransmission: Relevance for mood, mental state and memory. *Behavioural Brain Research* 105 (1999): 53–68.

Frances, Allen, and Michael B. First. *Your Mental Health: A Layman's Guide to the Psychiatrist's Bible*. New York: Scribner, 1998.

Frazer, Alan, Perry Molinoff, and Andrew Winokur (Eds.). *Biological Bases of Brain Function and Disease*. New York: Raven Press, Ltd., 1994.

Gould, Madelyn S., Ted Greenberg, Drew M. Velting, and David Shaffer. Youth suicide risk and preventive interventions: A review of the past 10 years. *Journal of the American Academy of Child and Adolescent Psychiatry* 42 (2003): 386 405.

Grucza, Richard A., Thomas R. Przybeck, and C. Robert Cloninger. Personality as a mediator of demographic risk factors for suicide attempts in a community sample. *Comprehensive Psychiatry* 46 (2005): 214–222.

Grunbaum, J.A., R. Lowry, L. Kann, and B. Pateman. Prevalence of health risk behaviors among Asian American / Pacific Islander high school students. *Journal of Adolescent Health* 27 (2000): 322–330.

Hales, Robert E., Stuart C. Yudofsky, and Robert H. Chew. *What Your Patients Need to Know About Psychiatric Medications.* Arlington, VA: American Psychiatric Publishing, Inc., 2005.

Health Maintenance Organization. (August 9, 2007). In *Wikipedia, The Free Encyclopedia.* Retrieved August 14, 2007, from *http://en.wikipedia.org/wiki/HMO.*

Janowsky, David S., Shirley Morter, and Liyi Hong. Relationship of Myers Briggs type indicator personality characteristics to suicidality in affective disorder patients. *Journal of Psychiatric Research* 36 (2002): 33–39.

Joe, S., R.E. Baser, G. Breeden, H.W. Neighbors, and J.S. Jackson. Prevalence of and risk factors for lifetime suicide attempts among Blacks in the United States. *Journal of the American Medical Association* 296 (2006): 2112–2123.

Johnson, Sharon L. *Therapist's Guide to Clinical Intervention: The 1-2-3's of Treatment Planning* (2nd ed.). San Diego, CA: Academic Press, 2004.

Kerby, Dave S. CART analysis with unit-weighted regression to predict suicidal ideation from Big Five traits. *Personality and Individual Differences* 35 (2003): 249–261.

Link, Bruce G., and Jo C. Phelan. Conceptualizing stigma. *Annual Review of Sociology* 27 (2001): 363–385.

Lopez, Roberto, and Jay Nagdimon (Eds.). *Suicide Prevention: Fighting for Life. Minorities Outreach Program. Agency Presenter's Guide.* Los Angeles, CA: Didi Hirsch Community Mental Health Center, 2001.

Maris, Ronald W., Alan L. Berman, and Morton M. Silverman (Eds.). *Comprehensive Textbook of Suicidology.* New York: The Guilford Press, 2000.

Mohler, Beat, and Felton Earls. Trends in adolescent suicide: Misclassification bias? *American Journal of Public Health* 91 (2001): 150–153.

National Research Council and Institute of Medicine. *Reducing Suicide: A National Imperative.* Committee on Pathophysiology & Prevention of Adolescent & Adult Suicide, Board on Neuroscience and Behavioral Health. Washington, DC: National Academy Press, 2002.

National Research Council and Institute of Medicine. *From Neurons to Neighborhoods: The Science of Early Child Development.* Committee on Integrating the Science of Early Child Development. In Jack P. Shonkoff and Deborah

A. Phillips (Eds.), Board on Children, Youth, and Families, Commission on Behavioral and Social Sciences and Education. Washington, DC: National Academy Press, 2000.

National Research Council and Institute of Medicine. *Nutrition During Pregnancy: Part II: Nutrient Supplements.* Subcommittee on Dietary Intake and Nutrient Supplements During Pregnancy, Committee on Nutritional Status During Pregnancy and Lactation, Food and Nutrition Board. Washington, DC: National Academy Press, 1990.

Pelletier, Kenneth R. *The Best Alternative Medicine: What Works? What Does Not?* New York: Simon & Schuster, 2000.

Phillips D.P., and T.E. Ruth. Adequacy of official suicide statistics for scientific research and public policy. *Suicide and Life Threatening Behavior* 23 (1993): 307–319.

Phoenix. (September 7, 2007). In *Wikipedia, The Free Encyclopedia.* Retrieved September 10, 2007, from http://en.wikipedia.org/wiki/Phoenix_%28mythology%29.

Pirkis, Jane E., Charles E. Irwin, Jr., Claire D. Brindis, Michael G. Sawyer, Christine Friestad, Michael Biehl, and George C. Patton. Receipt of psychological or emotional counseling by suicidal adolescents. *Pediatrics* 111 (2003): e388–e393.

Plous, Scott. *The Psychology of Judgment and Decision Making.* New York: McGraw-Hill, Inc., 1993.

Preferred Provider Organization (August 1, 2007). In *Wikipedia, The Free Encyclopedia.* Retrieved August 14, 2007, from http://en.wikipedia.org/wiki/Preferred_provider_organization.

Rockett, Ian R.H., Julie B. Samora, and Jeffrey H. Coben. The black–white suicide paradox: Possible effects of misclassification. *Social Science & Medicine* 63 (2006): 2165–2175.

Rubinow, David R., Peter J. Schmidt, and Catherine A. Roca. Estrogen–serotonin interactions: Implications for affective regulation. *Biological Psychiatry* 44 (1998): 839–850.

Sansone Family Center for Wellbeing. Temperament & Character Inventory. Available: https://psychobiology.wustl.edu/TCI/whatIsTCI.htm Accessed: September 14, 2007.

Saunders, Kate E. A., and Keith Hawton. Suicidal behaviour and the menstrual cycle. *Psychological Medicine* 36 (2006): 901–912.

Serotonin. (June 9, 2007). In *Wikipedia, The Free Encyclopedia.* Retrieved June 10, 2007, from http://en.wikipedia.org/wiki/Serotonin.

Shneidman, Edwin S. *The Suicidal Mind.* New York: Oxford University Press, 1996.

Sofronoff, Kate, Len Dalgliesh, and Robert Kosky. *Out of Options: A Cognitive Model of Adolescent Suicide and Risk-Taking.* New York: Cambridge University Press, 2005.

Snyder, C.R., and Shane J. Lopez (Eds.). *Handbook of Positive Psychology.* New York: Oxford University Press, 2005.

SSRI. (August 10, 2007). In *Wikipedia, The Free Encyclopedia.* Retrieved August 14, 2007, from http://en.wikipedia.org/wiki/SSRI.

Stigma. (n.d.). *Online Etymology Dictionary.* Retrieved September 14, 2007, from Dictionary.com Web site: *http://dictionary.reference.com/browse/stigma.*

Suicide Prevention Resource Center and Suicide Prevention Action Network. Suicide among American Indians / Alaska Natives. Available: *http://www.sprc.org/library/ai.an.facts.pdf* Accessed: September 14, 2007.

Suicide Prevention Resource Center and Suicide Prevention Action Network. Suicide among Asian American Indians / Pacific Islanders. Available: *http://www.sprc.org/library/asian.pi.facts.pdf.* Accessed: September 14, 2007.

Suicide Prevention Resource Center and Suicide Prevention Action Network. Suicide among Black Americans. Available: *http://www.sprc.org/library/black.am.facts.pdf.* Accessed: September 14, 2007.

Suicide Prevention Resource Center and Suicide Prevention Action Network. Suicide among Hispanic Americans. Available: *http://www.sprc.org/library/hispanic.am.facts.pdf* Accessed: September 14, 2007.

Traff, Catherine S. *The Calm Before the Storm: Recognizing When the Decision to Suicide Is Made.* Edmonton, Alberta: Turtle Pond Publishing, 2004.

U.S. Department of Health and Human Services. *Mental Health: A Report of the Surgeon General.* Rockville, MD: U.S. Department of Health and Human Services, 1999.

U.S. Department of Health and Human Services. *National Strategy for Suicide Prevention: Goals and Objectives for Action.* Rockville, MD: U.S. Department of Health and Human Services, 2001.

Van Heeringen, C., K. Audenaert, K. Van Laere, F. Dumont, G. Slegers, J. Mertens, and R.A. Dierckx. Prefrontal 5-HT$_{2A}$ receptor binding index, hopelessness and personality characteristics in attempted suicide. *Journal of Affective Disorders* 74 (2003): 149–158.

Wilson, John, and Marc Musick. The effects of volunteering on the volunteer. *Law and Contemporary Problems* 62 (2000): 141–168. Available: *http://www.law.duke.edu/shell/cite.pl?62+Law+Contemp.+Probs.+141+(Autumn+1999)* Accessed: September 14, 2007.

Index

Abilify (aripiprazole), 101
Access to lethal means, 42–43, 156
ACHA. *See* American College Health
    Association
Active Minds on Campus, 144, 171
Activities, supportive, 124, 145–46,
    147–48
Adolescent Mental Health Initiative
    (AMHI), xv
    web sites associated with, xvi
Adolescents
    child abuse/neglect's influence on,
        39–40, 40*t*–41*t*
    ethnicity and, 21, 22–23
    financial assistance for, 107–8
    positive psychology movement and,
        136–38
    psychotherapy adapted for, 89
    resources, support, for, xvi, 90–91,
        107–8, 171, 176, 177, 178, 179,
        180
    risk factors related to, 30–34, 38–44,
        40*t*–41*t*, 46–49
    sexual orientation and, 24*t*, 175
    suicidal thought/attempts statistics on,
        16–19, 21, 22–23, 24*t*
Advocacy, xx–xxiii
African Americans, 21–22
Alcoholics Anonymous, 132

Alcohol use, 28, 45, 48
    biological effects of, 67*t*–68*t*
    environmental risk factors and, 36–37,
        41*t*, 137
    for medicinal effect, 67, 67*t*–68*t*, 73
    suicide influenced by, 8, 68*t*
    as warning sign, 67, 67*t*–68*t*
Alprazolam (Xanax), 99
Alternative medicine, 105*t*
Ambien (zolpidem), 99
American College Health Association
    (ACHA), 17
AMHI. *See* Adolescent Mental Health
    Initiative
Anger/rage, 7*t*, 60, 64–65
Animal Assisted Therapy programs,
    128
Annenberg Foundation Trust at
    Sunnylands, xv, xxiii, 177
Anti-anxiety (anxiolytic) medication,
    98–99
Anticonvulsants, 102
Antidepressants, 95–98
    suicide risk associated with, 96*t*–97*t*,
        107
Antipsychotic medication, 100–101,
    102–3
Anxiety/agitation, 7*t*, 65, 98–99, 137
    medication as cause of, 96*t*–97*t*, 107

186